D0571479

Building Buzz to Beat
the Big Boys

Building Buzz to Beat the Big Boys

Word-of-Mouth Marketing for Small Businesses

Steve O'Leary and Kim Sheehan

DISCARDED

PRAEGER

Westport, Connecticut
London

BOWLING GREEN STATE
UNIVERSITY LIBRARIES

Library of Congress Cataloging-in-Publication Data

O'Leary, Steve.
   Building buzz to beat the big boys : word-of-mouth marketing for small businesses /
Steve O'Leary and Kim Sheehan.
      p. cm.
   Includes bibliographical references and index.
   ISBN 978-0-313-34598-2 (alk. paper)
   1. Word-of-mouth advertising.   2. Small business–Marketing.   I. Sheehan, Kim.
II. Title.
HF5827.95.044   2008
658.8'72—dc22   2007041080

British Library Cataloguing in Publication Data is available.

Copyright © 2008 by Stephen O'Leary and Kim Sheehan

All rights reserved. No portion of this book may be
reproduced, by any process or technique, without the
express written consent of the publisher.

Library of Congress Catalog Card Number: 2007041080
ISBN-13: 978-0-313-34598-2

First published in 2008

Praeger Publishers, 88 Post Road West, Westport, CT 06881
An imprint of Greenwood Publishing Group, Inc.
www.praeger.com

Printed in the United States of America

The paper used in this book complies with the
Permanent Paper Standard issued by the National
Information Standards Organization (Z39.48-1984).

10   9   8   7   6   5   4   3   2   1

To all the small business entrepreneurs who had the guts to start their own business knowing that their drive and determination could turn them from underdogs into champions.

Contents

Acknowledgments

We wish to thank our families, colleagues, and friends for their insights, their inspirations, and their encouragement during the course of this project. Thanks go to Tim Gleason, David Koranda, Alan Stavitsky, and Maki Kasumoto at the University of Oregon School of Journalism and Communication; Eric Anderson, Maria Migliore, Chollada Buathong, and the rest of the staff at O'Leary and Partners; Dr. Michael Foudy, Dr. Margaret Foley, and the staff at Foley Vision Center; Paige Sato at Modern Yarn; and Dylan Boyd at eROI. A huge thank you to our readers and advisors: Michael Todd, Amy Shepek, Ryan O'Leary, Mark O'Leary, Kasey O'Leary Massey, Jodi Schmidtgoesling, Chris Massey, Stan Wakefield, Jeff Olson, Tom Hunter, Glen Adams, Keith Galus, and Robin Miller.

Finally, our love and special thanks go our better halves, Patty O'Leary and Tim Sheehan.

Introduction

If you are holding this book in your hands right now, you are probably involved in some type of small business: You own a small retail store, you are a franchisee with a few outlets for a larger company, or you are a service provider. We know you are a very busy person, juggling the day-to-day running of your business with plans for its future growth. In addition, you are probably keenly aware of your competition, and if you have a spare moment here and there, wonder how you can differentiate yourself from your competition.

We know this book can help you.

This book grew out of our passion for wanting to help you, the small independent business owner. We wanted to give you some of the same benefits that the big chains have enjoyed in terms of marketing muscle: knowledge about advertising, marketing counsel, and some new ideas for you to try. We know you do not have the same marketing budgets that big chains do, but big budgets do not necessarily result in big ideas. Big ideas can come with limited budgets, and big ideas can have a big impact on your business.

The big chains do have a knowledge base derived from many years of experience where they have seen what has worked and what has not. This experience may help them see where things are heading in advertising and marketing today. We think we know where things are headed, and that is what we want to pass on to small business owners like you.

Between the two of us, we have been helping businesses, mostly large ones, with their advertising and marketing challenges for almost sixty years. We have built a lot of wisdom, and we have made our share of mistakes. We have worked for big advertising agencies in New York, Boston, Chicago, and Los

Angeles. We have done work for such mega-clients as McDonald's, Wendy's, Taco Bell, and Long John Silver's. We have handled assignments for huge manufacturers like Scott Paper, Standard Brands, Kraft, Miller Brewing, Coca-Cola, Minute Maid, and others. We helped in the marketing of big franchise chains as Century 21, Coldwell Banker, Fantastic Sam's, Uniglobe Travel, and Subway. We worked for banks, dry cleaning franchises, and other service businesses. We even worked for some special icons in their industries, like In-N-Out Burger. We are also entrepreneurs and teachers. We have started our own advertising agencies and consultancies, and we teach advertising to some of the brightest young minds in advertising today as well as some of the smartest street marketers you'll find out there. We think we're uniquely qualified to help you with your business.

So why did we want to write this book? Over the course of our careers, we have noticed that working for big companies isn't always what it's cracked up to be. We have learned what many of you learned. For one thing, big companies have many layers, and often it is difficult to find the person who can make the decision that can lead to the success of the brand. We have worked with many great brand managers at these companies, but we have also worked with brand managers who are really nothing more than brand babysitters. They do not manage for the success of the brand; instead, they micromanage the marketing process with the goal of making sure that nothing goes wrong. These brand babysitters are not risk takers, and they lack the entrepreneurial mindset to take their brands to the next level.

What we have found is that the people we like to work with are the people who are not afraid to take risks. Most of these people are entrepreneurs who have laid their personal assets on the line to start or buy a business. The real difference, though, is not the monetary investment they've made in their businesses. The real difference is the investment of their hearts and their souls into the success of their venture—the fact that they have a passion for what they're doing. If you have that passion, we share that passion with you.

Over the past several years, during the course of our work with our clients both big and small, we have noticed that the marketing environment is changing. While traditional advertising such as television, newspaper, and direct mail is still important to build awareness of your retail store or service business, it is no longer enough. In fact other types of marketing, specifically word-of-mouth marketing (WOM), is reemerging as a huge factor in consumer communications. The Internet is pushing this change in marketing to consumers and giving the consumer more control and choice. We have concluded that this change can provide the small business owner with an advantage over the big chains. How do you leverage this advantage? That is what this book is about. We believe that you, the small business owner and the entrepreneur, are best equipped to tailor your consumer message to meet your consumer's interests and needs. In doing so, you can create strong connections and ties with your customers, and they will become store champions for your business.

We wrote this book in order to give you the tools and techniques to create this dialogue with your consumers. Broadly, the two techniques we share are first, harnessing the power of word-of-mouth marketing, and second, creating a customer community. These techniques will help your store stand out of the clutter of advertising and marketing messages, and they will give you a terrific competitive advantage over your competitors big and small.

We wrote this book for anyone involved in a retail business or service, although we will use the term "retail store" as a catchall phrase throughout the book. You may have an advertising agency that you work with now, or you may do all of your own advertising and marketing. It is important for you to note that you do not need to hire an agency to create and implement word-of-mouth programs and customer communities. All you need is this book and the commitment to invest a bit of time and perhaps a bit of money in the process.

There is a basic roadmap to the process of creating word of mouth and customer communities, and it looks like this:

Customers → Conversations → Community → Commitment

We will start every chapter by showing you where we are on the roadmap. And then we will help you utilize the information in that chapter based on your current marketing activities and knowledge. After you finish reading this book, you will know:

- How to understand your customers better.
- How to increase customer loyalty to your store.
- How to communicate with customers to maintain their loyalty.
- How to encourage loyal customers to talk to others about your store.
- How to create a customer community, both in the store and online.
- How to maintain your commitment to this community.
- How to measure results.

We recognize that some of you may have dipped your toes in the waters of word-of-mouth marketing, while others of you may be complete novices. We have divided most of the chapters into three levels of information. The "Getting Started" section is for those of you who are completely unfamiliar with the concepts we are discussing. The "Moving Forward" is for those with a little bit of experience, and the "Taking It Further" section provides some of the most forward-thinking information on the topics today.

We know that you do not have a lot of time to spend on this information, and we hope this format makes it as easy for you to use as possible. You will also find a number of "Action Items" sprinkled throughout the chapters. If you are wondering how to get started or what the first steps should be for a particular effort, these action items will kick-start your activities and help you to focus on how to proceed. In addition, we have outlined some basic tools in the "Local Store

Toolbox" at the back of the book. This information will be helpful to those people with little experience in marketing.

At the end of many of our chapters, we will provide you with a "Resource Toolbox" with links to online references to give you more information or help you implement an action step. In addition, we have a companion Web site set up: www.underdognetwork.com. Why *underdog*? Because during our work with small businesses, we have often found that business owners feel like underdogs when competing against the big boys: the large chains and franchise operations that threaten to take over many markets and segments. But what do we know about underdogs? First, everyone roots for them, and second, they often come out on top. So our Web site, www.underdognetwork.com, is a place to meet other underdogs and learn from their experiences. We will also have a lot more information at the Web site about local store marketing. For example, we expand on the resource sections in the book by providing many more links to vendors that can help you with your business, we update our case studies, and we have a place where you can discuss the book and your own ideas on local store marketing with word of mouth and customer communities. You will also find our email addresses at the site if you need to get in touch with us. We hope you visit us online soon! We wish you the best of luck with your efforts.

Chapter **1**

The Importance of Word of Mouth and Customer Communities

Customers → Conversations → Community → Commitment

Customers today are faced with a myriad of choices, not only what to buy, but where to buy it. Complicating this choice is a "sea of sameness" in terms of products, services, and retail locations, which makes it difficult for customers to answer the question: "which one is best for me?" In this chapter, we introduce you to the concepts of word-of-mouth marketing and the value of customer communities and show you how to get started in envisioning these plans.

TODAY'S RETAIL ENVIRONMENT

When I need a haircut, how do I decide which one is the best for me? There are (approximately) 74,000 beauty salons in the United States. There are also about 4,000 barber shops and almost 9,000 nail salons.

What if I'm hungry? There are 195,412 full-service restaurants in the United States. There are even more quick-service restaurants. On top of that, there are 95,414 grocery stores, 9,451 coffee shops, and 48,855 bars. How do I decide which one to stop by?

There are 149,481 clothing stores in the United States. These stores are joined by 28,126 furniture stores, and 22,753 florists, all hoping to help me express my personal style. How do I know which is the best match for me?

That is a huge number of stores throughout the United States, and it represents a plethora of goods and services being sold. It is a crowded, busy, and possibly confusing situation for shoppers. Should they go to a "big box" merchant like Wal-Mart or Target, a regional chain, a small store, or should they just buy something online? As a retailer, you know it is incredibly hard to get your store to stand out. Can you stand out based on selection? Can you stand out based on price? Can you stand out based on customer service?

Maybe you can stand out to some degree in all of these areas. It is also likely that some of your competitors can claim these advantages. The chains can deliver on pricing, selection, and customer services. It means you have to compete on some other level. That is where this book comes in.

Your store can stand out against the competition by going to another level of personal connection to your customers, by building a unique and ongoing relationship with your customers, or what we call a "customer community." We will show you how to use word of mouth to build a customer community for your store. Using traditional research techniques, individual interactions with your customers, and word-of-mouth marketing, you will be able to confront your competition by nurturing and growing a loyal group of customers for your store. From that point, the possibilities are endless!

WHAT ARE WORD-OF-MOUTH MARKETING AND CUSTOMER COMMUNITIES?

Word-of-mouth marketing (WOM) is the process of information exchange, especially recommendations about products and services, between two people in an informal way. In the past, word of mouth has been a spoken phenomenon, but other types of dialogue (such as email and Web postings) are now included in the definition. It differs from other types of communication in that the source credibility is very high. That is, the person giving the information is generally seen as a much more credible source by the person receiving the information. This is especially true when someone knows the person that is giving him or her the information. A customer community is simply an organized system of customer contact. It is a system in which you have regular interactions with customers, both in person and electronically. This contact is personal, one on one, and recognizes that you understand the importance of each individual customer to your business. You share information and ideas with your customers, and you seek their input, feedback, and ideas in return. A customer community will be a hotbed for increased word-of-mouth advertising for your store.

WHAT CUSTOMER COMMUNITIES WILL DO FOR YOUR BUSINESS

We know you do not have a lot of time to invest in advertising and marketing. What's in it for you? Customer communities built through word of mouth have been shown to have numerous benefits for your business.

1. **A customer community will increase and reinforce customer loyalty.** If a customer takes it upon herself to tell a friend or colleague something positive about your store, it reinforces her own commitment to your business. Each time she tells her friends something positive about the store, she makes a commitment which validates and confirms her beliefs and feelings about your store. When she has another positive experience, she will start the cycle all over again. Additionally, the number of people she tells is a measure of the level of her loyalty. This increased loyalty occurs over time, and is based on the number of opportunities your loyal customer finds to praise your store. The more positive the experience, the more people will be told initially as well as the longer the individual will continue to pass on the good word.

2. **A customer community will improve business performance.** With each opportunity to talk about your store, your customer reminds herself of the positive experience. This significantly increases the chance that she will visit your store again soon. Customers who visit frequently spend more per visit and have higher ticket averages per person than those that visit infrequently. The lone exception to this might be shoppers who wait for sales.

   There is definitely a connection between word-of-mouth activities and long-term, total customer value. The frequent visitor is the one who is building an affinity for your store, and who is likely to have or make more opportunities to talk about your store to friends and family. Sometimes, though, the individuals like your store so much that they want to keep it a secret all to themselves. They need to be persuaded, in some way, to tell other people about your store. Your job, then, will be to encourage these folks to talk about your store. We will show you how in this book.

3. **A customer community will reduce marketing expenses.** Costs of promoting your store go down if you have a strong customer community. You may be able to reduce the amount of traditional advertising (radio, newspaper, television, and direct mail) that you currently do. Additionally, costs to open new locations may decrease.

4. **A customer community will insulate you from competition.** The more a customer is loyal to your store, the less likely he will be to switch to a competitor. It is a fact of life that some human beings crave new experiences, so even the most loyal customers may stop by a competitor to check it out once or twice. What you will find, though, is that your loyal customers are often using even a competitive experience to reinforce the fact that they made the right choice the first time.

5. **A customer community will increase your employee loyalty.** Happy customers who keep coming back result in a happy staff. Happy staff leads to more employee loyalty. Think of it as a circle. In a restaurant, for example,

WOM in Action: In-N-Out Burger is a regional chain of restaurants with incredibly loyal customers who love the restaurant for its simple menu, fresh ingredients, and great service. This loyalty is so strong that the chain does not have to advertise at levels equal to their competition. The chain has developed such a following, the loyal users often persuade visitors that they have to go to In-N-Out when visiting from out of town. Loyalists comment that once they begin talking about In-N-Out, the craving begins and they have to go right away. They have even created their own "secret menu" of ways that the basic menu can be modified or personalized. This has a great impact on the business. People start talking about a new In-N-Out store once they see it being built. A recent store opening in Arizona found people waiting outside the store for over twenty-four hours just to be one of the first to have an In-N-Out burger.

loyal customers are also usually better tippers than nonloyal customers are. They will refer friends to the restaurant, and these friends may even ask for the same server that serves the loyal customers. This reinforces the positive work that the server has provided. The new guest often comments on all the good things they have heard about the staff person, so the server gets more reinforcement that is positive.

WHY WORD-OF-MOUTH MARKETING IS SO POPULAR NOW

Word-of-mouth marketing has been around since a human first pointed to a cave painting to share the location of a good hunting ground with his family. You have probably heard the apocryphal statistic that a happy customer will tell one other person about a positive experience, but an unhappy customer will tell ten others about a negative experience. A recent study increased these numbers to 10 people for a good experience and 300 for a bad experience. That is probably due to people's desire to share what their experiences are increasing, and because the Internet facilitates that information exchange.[1]

People like to talk about shopping. A recent study by the Keller Fay Group found that Americans talk about products and services all the time. The average American discusses specific brands in ordinary discussion about eight times per day.[2] More than 60 percent of these brand talks feature products in a positive light. Almost half of these conversations refer to something the individual has seen in an ad or somewhere else in the media. People share information most often with family members and friends, and less often with colleagues. Since shoppers are already eager to talk about things that they buy, it is natural that marketers would reach out to harness that power. Today, some researchers say targeted word of mouth (that is positive word of mouth, not negative) is used by as many as 80 percent of companies.

Negative word of mouth is a hot topic in research circles today. A recent study by the Verde group,[3] for example, found that half of Americans experience a problem while shopping, and identified these as the top problems:

- The store did not have good parking.
- It took too long for customers to get in and out of the store.
- Customers found it hard to find products.
- The store layout and displays were confusing.
- The front-line staff had poor product knowledge or lacked courtesy.

About a third of these people tell one or more friends about the specific problem they experienced, and on average, they tell four people. Now, among those four people who are told about the problem, two of them will never step foot in the store that their friend told them about. In addition, it is likely that these two friends will tell other friends about the problem.

WHY YOU SHOULD HARNESS THE POWER OF WORD OF MOUTH

One thing we stress throughout this book is talking to your customers: finding out their likes, dislikes, and their ideas on how to make shopping in your store better. The Verde study found that dissatisfied shoppers are five times more likely to complain to friends than to the retailer.

We recommend that you do not wait to hear about bad things (or good things for that matter) from your customers. Talk to them! This is one of the important steps you need to undertake when creating word of mouth. Ask your customer in person if everything met their expectations. And try to ask this in an open-ended way—not a question that can be answered with *yes* or *no* but a question that gives you more insight as to your customers' feelings. Ask, for example:

- What else would you like to see at our store?
- What would make your experience better?

WOM in Action: One of the most successful new businesses in recent history is a company called BzzAgent. David Balter founded BzzAgent in 2001. The company matches its client companies with products or services to promote with individuals all across the United States who are interested in promoting products. These individuals sign on as volunteers, review the clients' products and services to be promoted, and select the clients that they wish to talk about. They then receive information about the products and services they select, and conduct additional research on their own to create the messages that they tell to friends, family, and colleagues. The individuals report their conversations in the form of a bzzreport. For every bzzreport they complete, individuals receive points that are redeemable for prizes. By all accounts, BzzAgent is an incredibly successful company, recently garnering a $13.75 million series B round of funding and gaining clients including Anheuser-Busch, Lee Jeans, and Cadbury Schweppes.[4]

These initial customer conversations are incredibly important. Review the negative word-of-mouth situations identified above and think about how just knowing the problems existed could have led to the problem being corrected. And that would result in a decrease in the negative word of mouth.

WORD OF MOUTH AND THE LOCAL STORE ADVANTAGE

As a local store marketer, you have a resource that the big box stores and other chains do not have: the ability to have constant, personal interaction with your customers. This book is for all types of retail marketers and small business owners who work for or own stores that provide all types of goods and services. The best plan you can develop is one that is unique to your store and meaningful for your customers. You know best what makes your store unique. It may be your product mix, your excellent service, your premium location, or your prices. It may be the special offerings that you provide. Identifying your unique qualities will help you decide what will be the content of your conversations with your customers. When you tell others something interesting, there is a good chance that they will tell someone else about it. This book will help you do that.

HOW A CUSTOMER COMMUNITY FITS INTO YOUR ADVERTISING PLAN

You probably have some type of marketing plan established for your store. As you will learn in the next few chapters, you will want to integrate your word of mouth and community activities into your traditional advertising activities. Thus, you might wish to begin by plotting out your planned marketing activities for the next year. If you have never done this, visit the Toolbox section in the back of the book for an illustration of setting up this marketing grid. When you are done reading this book, your marketing grid might look something like this.

All of this will be made clear as you move through the book, and having a single place to organize your plans and ideas will be very helpful in making sense of all this information and keeping in mind the big picture of what you're planning to do.

SUMMING UP

Before you move on to the next chapter, we hope you:

- Realize how important word of mouth, both positive and negative, is to your business.
- Understand that you can control word of mouth and that it has benefits to you.

Table 1-1 Marketing Grid

Month	Promo	Media	Word of Mouth: Target	Word of Mouth: Activity	Community: Target	Community: Activity
January						
Week 1	End of year	N	Family	Email about final clearance specials		
Week 3				Valentine's Day sneak peek		
Week 4	Valentine's	N			Message board	How do you celebrate Valentine's Day?
February						
Weeks 1–2	Valentine's	R	Friends and Flirts	Send Valentine's Day cards		
March						
Week 2			Store Champions	Referral event: spring trend fashion show	Message board	What's your must-have accessory for spring?
Weeks 3–4	Easter	R, N	Family	Poll: what summer items are you thinking about?		

- Take advantage of these benefits and begin to see how word of mouth will
  - Increase customer loyalty.
  - Improve business performance.
  - Reduce marketing expenses.
  - Insulate you from competition.
  - Improve employee loyalty.
- Start looking for ways to include word of mouth into your marketing plans.

The next step is start understanding your customers better and find ways to learn more about them. That is what we will cover in Chapter 2.

Chapter **2**

Who Are Your Customers?

Customers → Conversations → Community → Commitment

This chapter is about your customers, specifically about figuring out what you know, what you do not know, and how to fill in the gaps. The focus of this investigation is your market and your customers. This information will be used to figure out how to best use word-of-mouth marketing and how to develop a customer community. But first things first! In the Getting Started sections, we will provide an overview of the basic information you need to get started. The Toolbox has more detailed information on how to do this basic research if you've never done this. Then we will Move Forward with a discussion of demographics. Finally, we will show you how to analyze and use this information to segment customers in the Taking It Further Section.

GETTING STARTED: DEFINING YOUR TRADING AREA BY GEOGRAPHY AND ZIP CODES

Do you know who your customers are? Of course, you do—you see them on a regular basis patronizing your store. But how well do you know them? What do you know about them? Do you know where they live? How often do they shop in your store? What do they like best about your store? What are some things they do not like? Perhaps most important: What, if anything, do they tell others about your store? A complete and thorough knowledge of your customers, inside and out, is essential to learning how to create a community of loyal patrons. We need to know a lot, but it is not as difficult as it might seem. For instance, the basic information that we need is the ZIP code that they live in, their frequency of visits, what things do they purchase most often, what do they like best about your store. We will show you how to capture and use this information.

But we are getting ahead of ourselves here. Knowing your customers both current and new is critical in many areas to making your store a success. This chapter is dedicated to understanding your customer from several perspectives. You have probably already used this information to select the right location for your store, to know which specific demographic groups you should concentrate on, and to know which products and services you should feature in your store. We will show you how to build upon this information to best understand your customers today.

It is important to remember that today's consumer is different from your customer of five years ago. Customers today want more information. They want to be more involved in their purchase decisions. They look for services and products specifically designed for them. And last, they want opportunities to provide feedback to the store owner, and, once they give that feedback, to know that you are using it to make your store a better place for them to visit.

The bottom line is: You can no longer rely on doing some initial research that you use in developing your local store marketing plan and then leave it at that. Today, you must constantly monitor who your customers are, what they are purchasing, and most important, how they feel about your store. Once this baseline is established, you can move on to developing customers that are more loyal, more word-of-mouth activities for your store, and a greater sense of community among your customers.

So let us start with identifying your trading area. Your local trading area, also known as your retail trade area, is where your customers live. Simple, yes?

By definition, a local trading area is the geographic area that generates the majority of the customers for a community, a business district, or downtown area. Knowing the boundaries of your own retail trade area is helpful in that it helps you estimate the total number of potential customers that you have and where they live. It will also allow you to compare the profile of your current customer to the profile of the resident of the retail trading area.

In some cases, the boundaries of your retail trade area are the same as the boundaries of your local community. In other cases, though, your trade area will be much smaller than the boundaries of your community. A gas station's trade area, for example, tends to be a small radius of the neighborhood around the station. Some trade areas are larger than the boundaries of your community. That is, people will travel a long distance to visit your establishment. People travel farther to visit a furniture store than they do to the dry cleaners. So the frequency of visits or purchase cycle influences the size of the trading area.

If you've been running your store for a while, you probably have a general idea of the geographic area that your local trade area encompasses. Two tools, Reilly's Law of Retail Gravitation and ZIP Code Tabulation, will allow you to define this a bit further.

> **WOM in Action:** The Center for Economic Development at the University of Wisconsin suggests that while every store has its own unique trading area, all retail trading areas can be generalized into two different types: convenience shopping trade areas and comparison shopping trade areas.[1] The convenience shopping trade area is based on the ease of access to convenience products such as food and gas: That is, people will decide where they will buy the products (i.e., which specific store) based on travel distances or travel time. Grocery stores and gas stations are among these types of stores.
>
> Comparison shopping trade areas are based on price, selection, quality, and style. Shoppers may visit several stores as well as travel farther to compare offerings for products and service in these categories. Appliance and furniture stores are traditional examples of these types of stores. Convenience is still the primary motivator for restaurants, beauty salons, and other personal-service businesses. However, because it is a personal service or has high level of importance in the consumer's mind, convenience can be overcome by the quality of the experience or a tie to a particular service person. Beauty salon stylists often have customers follow them from salon to salon and even travel many miles to keep using them.

Reilly's Law of Retail Gravitation

Reilly's Law of Retail Gravitation is based on the premise that people are attracted to large places to do their shopping, but the time and distance they must travel influences their willingness to shop at any given store. For example, I may like that new bookstore across the river at the mall, but I am just as happy to shop at the local college bookstore closer to my house. It is a fact of life that people will travel shorter distances whenever possible. However, people are more likely to shop at places where there are many different things to buy. That explains why the bakery at the mall may be more successful than the bakery with the better pastries four blocks from the mall. The density of population in the area will also affect patronage of your store. The more people living in an area, the tighter the convenience ring is around the store.

Visit our Local Store Toolbox in the Appendix at the back of the book for specific instructions on creating your own map. We also provide a visual illustration of what your map might look like. Reilly's Law provides a general sense of where your community's trade areas are and an approximation of your store's local trading area, but does not take into account individual shopping patterns. That is where the next method, ZIP Code Tabulation, comes in handy.

ZIP Code Tabulation

Whenever I shop at a certain bed and bath store, the salesperson always asks for my ZIP code at the checkout counter. This store is using ZIP Code Tabulation to analyze their market area. ZIP Code Tabulation is a superior method to Reilly's Law since it uses real data to identify your retail trade area. Visit our

Local Store Toolbox in the Appendix for instructions on how to use ZIP Code Tabulation at your store.

Once you have this data based on ZIP codes, you can use it in several different ways. If you know other retailers who use this method, you can compare your data to theirs to have an even better understanding of your market. Or you can compare the data from two different retail outlets that you operate to get a better handle on market opportunities.

Another thing you can do with this information is evaluate the efficiency of your current traditional advertising schedule (if you have one). For example, you may find through your calculations that almost half your customers live in a single ZIP code. Your map may provide you with this same conclusion. Experience indicates that more often than not the ZIP code you are located in ends up being where the bulk of your customers come from. But you need to perform this analysis to be sure.

MOVING FORWARD: DETERMINING THE DEMOGRAPHICS OF YOUR TRADING AREA

Now that you know your trading area, you can ask yourself the critical question of just who lives in your retail trading area. Specifically, you want to know the concentrations of different types of people who might have different purchasing behaviors. The basic demographic information that you will be looking at is total population and the age, income, and ethnicity of people in the area. You'll also want to know about whether they have kids or not, and whether they own or rent their home. Visit the Toolbox in the back of this book for much more information about demographics.

This information is incredibly useful, as demographics influence purchase behaviors. Older people have different shopping patterns than younger people. People with kids shop differently than people without kids. Homeowners buy different things than renters. Understanding these differences and knowing what differences exist in your local trade area gives you a leg up in marketing your store.

You can find several services you can use to help you understand the types of people who live in your neighborhood. Detailed local census data are readily available free via the Internet through the U.S. Bureau of Census. Census data can be retrieved at several geographic levels (county, city/village, town, census tract, ZIP code, etc.).

In addition to the Census Bureau, several private sources can help you learn about the customers in your retail trading area. Private data firms can provide estimates for particular trade areas; look in your local Yellow Pages or do an online search for different data and research firms that are available. You can also check with direct mail companies in your area, who can provide a detailed breakdown of the makeup of consumers in your area. Our Web site, www.underdognetwork.com, has a list of some of these companies. Your local direct mail reps may also have this information.

Action Idea: You can access the Census Bureau as your primary resource for determining the demographics of your trading area. Access to the Census is available free via the Internet at a Web site called American FactFinder (factfinder.census.gov/home/saff/main.html). This user-friendly site will let you view, print, and download statistics about population, housing, industry, and business. The Basic facts section provides fast answers to common questions about population size. In addition, this feature allows you to find statistical information for many geographic areas and display the data in a table or on a map.

While finding these data is important, interpretation of the data is key. As you review the demographic information that you obtain, consider what the data are saying about your market: Is it changing? How are people spending their time? Their money? If you're unfamiliar with basic information about demographics, visit the Toolbox in the back of this book. Demographic statistics are especially useful when you can compare them to other demographics. To see how your retail trade area is unique, you can compare your retail trade area to the larger community, other communities, or your state. You can pinpoint exactly what makes your trade area different: You may have more families with children or more blue-collar workers.

You are now armed with lots of information, which can help you fine-tune your current marketing efforts. By knowing your area, it will lead you to developing special marketing efforts to specific groups of consumers. For example, if you have a large concentration of families, you may market to them differently than you would market a group of young adults. If you had a clothing store you would market different clothes to the segments. If you had a restaurant, you offer different meals to families versus young adults. You might also consider seniors as important customers. You may have a special seniors effort, for example, providing them with special pricing, shopping at special times of the day, and special offers or products designed specifically for them. If you have a high concentration of a language group, you may need to have special menus or price sheets in the appropriate language of that consumer group. You may even need to have a special sales staff that speaks the language.

TAKING IT FURTHER: LOOKING AT YOUR BUSINESS BY CUSTOMER SEGMENTS

Demographics are a fine way to segment your audience. You can segment customers demographically—that is, by age, gender, or race. A hair salon, for example, would have a different communication strategy for men than for women since women spend much more on average at a salon than men. Men have their hair cut more often and thus visit more frequently, but are driven more by convenience. Women visit less often, and their past experiences with the salon and the stylist are important drivers for their return.

But the most interesting part of the process comes next. You want to move on to looking at your customers by segments based on their purchasing behavior. These segments go beyond knowing how to describe your customers and into what makes them want to visit your store and shop there. Such information includes consumer perceptions about the benefits and values of your store as well as the motivations to shop at your store or at other locations.

Once you collect this data about many of your customers, you will be able to segment them into different groups based on these attitudes. In a nutshell, customer segmentation is the idea that all customers are not alike, but some customers share similarities with other customers. If you can identify different groups of customers that share something in common, it is possible to also identify and create communications, promotions, and rewards that are most appropriate for them. You can also understand whether they are likely to tell others about their experiences in your store, and you can use this information to find ways to stimulate word-of-mouth activity among them.

YOUR LOYALTY SEGMENTS: THE FAMILY, FLIRTS, AND PHANTOMS

We will focus much of the information in this book using loyalty segments. We divide store customers into three segments based on their loyalty to the store. What is loyalty? You are probably most familiar with the idea of brand loyalty, such as "I am a loyal Coke drinker," or "I am a loyal Toyota purchaser." Although you hear brand loyalty most often attached to a specific product, there is no reason why your retail store cannot be a brand also.

What is a brand? A brand is a combination of several different things. It is the actual brand name, such as Coke or Toyota or Macy's or Nordstrom's. In addition, it is the image that comes to a consumer's mind when he or she thinks about the brand. It includes whether customers perceive the brand is exciting or conservative, fashionable or nerdy. For many products and services, the brand is its main competitive advantage.

Michael Porter, a Harvard University professor and an expert on company strategy and competition, defines competitive advantage as when a company is able to deliver the same benefits as its competitor but at a lower cost, or when a company can deliver benefits that exceed those of a competing product. Nordstrom's competitive advantage, then, is service. Toyota's is dependability. Depending on how important the competitive advantage is to your customers, it can be a key driver of brand loyalty.

Brand loyalty is built when customers perceive that a brand offers a competitive advantage through the right product features, images, and/or quality level at the right price. Your retail store has a name and you may or may not have a recognizable logo. Your store name becomes a brand when customers have perceptions on the attributes and benefits of your store. Determinants of brand loyalty, then, will be unique for different groups of customers based on their perceptions. Their level of brand loyalty, whether they have high or low loyalty, will be based upon your customer's conscious or unconscious decision to continually patronize your store for specific products or services. This decision can be an actual behavior (i.e., they are continually shopping at our store) or an intention (a statement that they plan to continually shop at your store).

Attributes of your store are the things your store has or does. These include information relative to the location of your store and how convenient it is to your customers, the types of products or services that you sell, how people pay for items, how your store is laid out, the level of customer service, your hours of operation, and the like. Attributes turn into benefits when they become meaningful to your customers, particularly your loyal customers. Benefits of your store are based on the customers' perceptions of what your store provides to them relative to other choices. This can include perceptions of convenience ("I can get what I need and be on my way quickly"), perceptions of quality ("I am treated like a queen at this shoe store"), and perceptions of value ("This store makes me feel like a smart shopper"). All of your specific attributes and benefits can work together to develop loyalty, and they all come down to the fact that the customer had an enriching experience in your store (both in real life and online).

The benefits to loyalty are overwhelming. Customer loyalty to your store, your brand, allows you to maintain a strong position in the market. With loyal customers, their spending tends to accelerate over time. Loyal customers have fewer problems with operations, and they are less price-sensitive than newer customers.[2] Because their spending accelerates, and because you will not have to invest in a lot of advertising to keep them coming to the store, one consulting group suggested that a 5 percent increase in a company's retention rates will increase the average lifetime profits per customer.[3] Most important, though, loyal customers are more likely than any other type of customer to tell others about your store.[4]

We need to make something crystal clear: Not every customer is going to be a loyal customer. This is just a fact of life. That does not mean you totally forget about them. What is important is that you think about your customers based on loyalty as falling into one of three different groups. Understanding these groups will help you figure out the right mix of promotions that will maximize your business. Additionally, as we start to talk more about word of mouth, we will see that people in the groups are likely to respond differently to your efforts.

But first, we would like to introduce you to the three segments that represent three different levels of loyalty to your store: the Family, the Flirts, and the Phantoms.

The Family

Have you ever heard the old adage that 10 to 20 percent of your customers account for 70 to 80 percent of your business? This rule of thumb is known as the

Pareto principle. In many product descriptors, these people are called the heavy users, *heavy* not referring to their weight but to their purchase frequency. We prefer to call them the Family: the customers that are very loyal to your store. Statistically, when they are choosing between other retail stores that sell similar items to yours, they will select your store more than 75 percent of the time. As we have said, they are motivated by a unique mix of attributes and benefits found at your store.

If customers are considered Family, it is likely that the salespeople or waiters recognize them when they walk in the store. The customers indicate to those in the store that they like the store, know some of your salespeople by name, and stop to chat during a transaction. Customers feel like they are part of your store; they have an affinity for the store and simply enjoy the experience of going to and spending time there.

It used to be that the most loyal customers tended to be older, affluent customers. However, a recent study by the AARP found that brand loyalty does not increase with age, and older customers are just as likely to be Flirts or Phantoms than younger customers are.

There is an important subset of the Family: The members of your Family who are motivated primarily by convenience. Convenience is defined as how easy it is to shop at the store based on how close it is to the customer's home or workplace. This subset, the Extended Family, is loyal to your store but may be more open to switching to another option if a competitive store opens closer to them. Examples are customers of neighborhood grocery stores and dry cleaners. The customers are loyal because they can visit these stores on the way to or home from work or school.

With the Family, it is important in your research to find out the unique mix of attributes and related benefits that makes them loyal to your store. You need to constantly remind and reinforce these benefits to these loyal customers, so loyalty to your store can be constantly maintained. Additionally, if these are important attributes and benefits that may resonate with people other than the Family, you may be able to leverage these among other groups to increase their patronage.

You should chat with Family members often to find out what they're thinking and what they like and dislike about your store so you will know how to maintain their loyalty. Even brands with strong customer loyalty have to maintain this relationship, by continuing to provide the mix of attributes and benefits required by your customers. Remember, people change and evolve, and you must respond to these changes with changes in your store.

The Flirts

The Flirts are customers that shop at both your store and your competitors' stores. They are likely to represent about 50 percent of your customers and between 20 and 30 percent of your income. Many Flirts tend to be loyal to good prices and have the time, energy and inclination to shop around and find the best values and deals on the products and services that they want and need. Flirts may also have a group of stores that are in their decision set that they check out before making a purchase. However, you will want to confirm both these things by talking with members of this group.

Understanding the unique motivations of the Flirts will help you figure out how to increase their purchasing frequency at your store. Some Flirts may become loyal, but other Flirts may simply enjoy being Flirts. That does not mean that you do not pay attention to them. Instead, you have to think about the unique role Flirts play in your retail community.

Flirts shop around. They are variety and deal seekers. They know a lot about the products, services, and retailers in your community, and they are possibly experts in variety of the offerings at your store and at your competitor's stores. As experts, they are likely to talk to others about their findings.

Basically, they are important prospects for word-of-mouth campaigns, which we will talk about in the next several chapters. To sum up, once Flirts become more loyal, you can encourage them to become powerful word-of-mouth champions for your store.

The Phantoms

They live within your trading area, they share the same demographic traits as the Family and the Flirts, but the Phantoms are different—you almost never see them. To put it bluntly, customers in this segment are not loyal to your store. Phantoms represent a large portion of your trading area, but a very small portion of your sales. For example, they may make up 30 to 40 percent of your customer base, but only account for about 10 percent of your store's sales.

There are several reasons why someone is a Phantom:

- They may not be aware of your store and therefore have never visited it.
- They may be aware of your store but are not interested in shopping there, so they also have not visited.
- They may be part of the Family at another store, and so are infrequent visitors to your store.
- They may have been either part of your Family or even a Flirt but something happened to persuade them not to visit your store again.

Let us think about each of these groups of Phantoms individually.

The Phantom may not be aware of your store, and has never visited. If the Phantom has a route to work that does not go by your store, and she does not read the newspaper or the direct mail pieces you have sent, and she does not listen to one of the four radio stations that run your commercials, she may simply not be aware of your store. Mixing up your advertising schedule by running ads at different times and trying a few new media vehicles may take care of this problem. More ideas on attracting these types of Phantoms with advertising and other marketing techniques can be found at our Web site, www.underdog network.com.

The Phantom may be aware of your store but has never shopped there. The Phantom may know your store is there but is simply not interested in shopping at your store. Basically, she does not have the information she needs to make a decision to shop at your store. A detailed direct-marketing piece, outlining some of the key products and services that you offer, may make an impact.

> **Action Idea:** A small, family-owned drug-and-variety store runs a full-page ad on the back of the weekly TV guide, and fills the ad with more than fifty different products that are on sale that week (the ad often features seasonal products at full price with a few other products on special). The ad also reinforces some of the services they offer (such as a post office, pharmacy, and photo developing studio). The net result is the idea that this store, which many customers see as a small store in comparison with other drug stores, offers tons of stuff for sale. So if a shopper needs something—anything—they might as well stop at the store and see if they have it.

The Phantom may be part of the Family at another store. Remember from our earlier definition of the Family that someone who considered himself or herself part of a store's Family chooses that store about 70 percent of the time. There is an opportunity there. It is rare to find someone who spends all of their money on any specific type of item at only one store. Think about trying to get a bit of the share of wallet from this Phantom. The key to addressing this type of Phantom is not only knowing what he wants, but what his current Family does not provide. Is there anything that you offer through your business that your competitor does not offer?

The Phantom was once either a Family member or a Flirt but something happened to persuade them not to visit your store again. In this case, it is important for you to learn what exactly happened. This Phantom could have had a bad service experience, she might think your prices are too high, or she looked for something in your store and could not find it—so she went to another store. Regardless, she has not come back.

This is the subsegment of Phantoms that most retailers think they should not pursue. A study by the White House Office of Consumer Affairs once reported that 91 percent of dissatisfied customers will never purchase from the offending company again. Now, that is a good reason not to go after the Phantoms, but it may be a myth. Time heals all wounds, and the strong dislike once registered for your store may fade over time. We as human beings have a strong capacity to forgive and forget. Use your customer research to help you understand how to reach out to these customers.

Table 2-1 Summary of Family, Flirts, and Phantoms

	% of Customers	*% of Sales*	*Keys to Your Business*
Family	10–20%	60–80%	Heavy word of mouth Monitor happiness constantly
Flirts	40–50%	20–30%	Experts who talk to a lot of people Great source for starting word of mouth
Phantoms	30–40%	10% or less	Make them aware store is there Fix any problems quickly

The importance of the Phantoms leads to a key idea for customer research: You cannot only research the customers who are currently in your store. If you do that, you will not get an idea of what the Phantoms are thinking.

So there they are: the Family, the Flirts, and the Phantoms. See Table 2-1 for a chart to help you remember their roles and importance to your business.

GETTING THE DATA ABOUT YOUR CUSTOMERS

As you can see from the previous section, there is a lot you want to learn about your customers that you cannot get from published demographic data. You want to learn their likes and dislikes so that you can adjust your services and marketing to meet their changing desires. You can use a number of different techniques to talk to the Family and the Flirts, and there are even ways you can reach out to the Phantoms to learn more about them.

The other reason you want to talk to your customers is that this is the first step into generating a word-of-mouth campaign. You want to get customers used to talking about your business as part of their normal conversations. And while a survey or a poll would not be considered a normal conversation, you are moving the topic of your store up the relevance ladder for your customers. There is no guarantee that they will start talking about your store, but it is an important start that you need to take.

Finding out what your consumers think is something you should be doing on a regular basis; and we recommend that you conduct some type of customer research every six months at a minimum. Keep in mind, though, that some consumers openly do not like to be contacted. If you ask someone to participate and he or she refuses, do not badger the individual, and just leave it at that. However, do not be deterred by consumers who do not want to be contacted. Reach out to those consumers who are interested in helping you improve your store. Be sure to make the purpose of your research very clear, and tell them that their input will be used to improve the service and offerings at your location.

To begin this process, first consider how often you think you will be able to conduct the type of consumer research we have been talking about in this chapter. Think about the nature of your specific business: Are there times during the year when you are less busy? That might be a good time to conduct research (it will also remind consumers that you are around, and that might bring them in for a visit). Additionally, you will want to think about what type of research method you will use.

Selecting Your Methodology

There are five basic techniques you can use to talk to your customers: phone surveys, card surveys, online surveys, focus groups/group discussions, and inter-cept/personal surveys done in local malls. We describe each of these techniques in our Toolbox section and give you some information on what works well with these techniques and what some of the negative aspects are. However, please note that customer research is both a science and an art, and entire books and Web sites are devoted to the practice and analysis of consumer data. We have provided some links at the end of the chapter to give you a few more resources to learn about your selected method.

Once you start the process of talking to customers, you may start to feel over-whelmed by information. How do you begin to understand all that the customers are telling you? You will want to start by tabulating responses to any type of scale questions, as well as reading through all the open-ended comments that your respondents provide. As you review these data, think about the results using these guiding questions:

- What do people like about us?
- What do people like about our competitors?
- What can we do to improve our business?

Armed with this information, you will want to develop an action plan for the next six months based on these data. You probably will not be able to implement all the things that your customers tell you that they want, and in fact you should not. Instead, try to gauge what are the key things that keep coming up repeat-edly from your customers. Do they want longer hours? Do they want more infor-mation about the products you offer? Do they need lower prices? Think of the one or two things that you read repeatedly in your data, and then decide on an action plan based on those things.

Whenever you make a change based on customer input, think of ways to inform your customers that you have listened to them and acted on their recommendations. How do you do this? For service businesses, think about table talkers or a sign that tells the customers about the changes. Perhaps your employees could wear a button that says "we listened!" You might even want to think about starting a newsletter to keep people informed on what is happening in the store. (We will talk more about that in the next few chapters.)

What is important to remember, though, is that these actions do more than announce a change. These are important tools to start a dialogue with customers—an ongoing conversation about your store that will help keep it top of mind with your customers. This dialogue is key to getting your customers to start talking about your store to others.

SUMMING UP

In this chapter, we have shown you:

- How to think about your customers and your marketplace using several different techniques.
- How to consider your current customers in terms of three key segments: the Family, the Flirts, and the Phantoms.
- Why different customers end up being in one of these segments, and what you need to do to connect with each segment.
- That research is more than a cost of doing business. Research is the way that you can create personal relationships with customers.
- Why you need to begin a dialogue with your customers.

Online or offline, in your store or in the mall, these dialogues are the first step in enhancing relationships with your customers. These types of relationships will lead to valuable word of mouth for your store. And in the next chapter, we will tell you all about that.

RESOURCE TOOLBOX

At our Web site (www.underdognetwork.com), we have links to many sites and tools to help you with your research. Here are a few to get you going.

- To learn more about focus groups: www.managementhelp.org/evaluatn/focusgrp.htm, www.groupsplus.com/pages/mn091498.htm.
- To learn more about mall intercepts: www.busreslab.com/articles/article4.htm.
- To learn more about online surveys: freeonlinesurveys.com, www.websurveyor.com/features.asp?ref=gppc:1488, www.surveymonkey.com.

Chapter **3**

Getting Started with Word of Mouth

Customers → *Conversations* → Community → Commitment

By now, you have learned a lot about your customers. That is a terrific base of knowledge to have. You have also begun a dialogue with your customers by finding out what they like and do not like about your store. Hopefully, you have made a change or two to improve your business, and you are seeing the results. Maybe you have let your customers know about the change. All of these steps are important beginnings to develop that important tool: word of mouth. Word of mouth is basically conversations, and the fact that you are in the process of establishing a dialogue, a conversation, with your customers is important. However, asking them to pass along information to others is the heart of word of mouth.

This chapter is all about those conversations. The Getting Started section is for those who are unfamiliar with word of mouth. It describes the recent history and theory behind this powerful tool. If you are ready to start with word of mouth, skip to the Moving Forward section. And if you feel comfortable that you have a positive word-of-mouth effort organized for your store, skip to the Taking It Further section, which introduces a customer segmentation plan that we have developed.

GETTING STARTED: BACKGROUNDS, DEFINITIONS, AND HISTORY OF WORD OF MOUTH

Have you ever read a great book or seen a great movie, and could not wait to tell someone about it? Or what about the last time you went to a great new restaurant? Were you jumping out of your chair wanting to tell your friends about the place you went to and how great the food and service was? This chapter is about understanding this phenomenon. We want to help you find ways to re-create this experience on a regular basis with your customers as they visit your store.

What gets customers talking? Many things. A research company, GkfNOP, recently surveyed American consumers to find out just what, exactly, led to the start of a word-of-mouth campaign. And here were the answers:

- 50 percent of the survey respondents said that advertising in magazines and on television and in-store activities led them to make a recommendation for a product or service to someone they knew.
- 50 percent also said that in-store activities (such as a demonstration or special in-store event) started them in word of mouth.
- Almost 50 percent of the respondents said that a coupon or discount got them talking.
- More than 30 percent said that something they saw on the Web got the tongues wagging.
- About 30 percent told others about a free sample.
- 18 percent forwarded an email to someone they knew.[1]

In the retail marketing context, Emanuel Rosen believes that word of mouth can be considered oral communication about products and services with friends, family, and colleagues.[2] Rosen also suggests that word of mouth leads to buzz. He defines *buzz* as the "sum of all comments about a particular product or company at a certain point in time."

The key component to Rosen's definition is the idea of a *comment*—a thought, an idea, a message, or an opinion that is transferred from one person to another. You want to have a dialogue with your customers. They have opinions and they want to share them. They want you to hear them and respond. This is the key to developing a two-way communication that will create positive word of mouth.

All your customers have opinions: about your store location, your offerings, and your service. In many cases, these opinions will be positive ones. Occasionally there may be negative ones. That is just an unpleasant fact. To harness the power of word of mouth that we described in the first chapter, though, you need to know if customer opinions are positive or negative. You learned that from the research you conducted that we described in Chapter 2.

JUST WHAT IS WORD OF MOUTH?

Is word-of-mouth marketing (WOM) the same as buzz marketing? What about "shill" marketing? If they are different, how are they different, and what type is best for you? We need to understand definitions because we need to be clear about what type of WOM we are trying to create and how it can be created in order to have the greatest benefit on your store. There are different types and styles of WOM and they have different effects on your business. The Word of

Mouth Marketing Association (WOMMA) has recently begun a campaign to formalize definitions of these types of activities.

WOMMA has defined word of mouth as "the act of a consumer creating and/or distributing marketing-relevant information to another consumer."[3] For a retail store, then, marketing-relevant information would be any type of information about your store that would lead a consumer to come to visit your store. Additionally, WOMMA defines word-of-mouth marketing as an effort by an organization to affect how consumers create and/or distribute marketing-relevant information to other consumers. And just to be helpful, they provide an alternative definition: "An effort by an organization to encourage, facilitate and amplify marketing relevant communication among consumers."[4]

So just to clarify, word of mouth is something that your customers do. Word of mouth marketing is something that you do to encourage your customers to talk to other customers about your store.

Researcher Walter Carl identified two types of word of mouth: "everyday word of mouth" and "institutional" word of mouth.[5] Carl defines everyday word of mouth as an informal, evaluative communication that takes place between at least two conversational participants about characteristics of an organization and/or a brand, product, or service. Institutional word of mouth is word-of-mouth communication in which the institutional identity or corporate affiliation of at least one participant is prominent, and/or where the organization, brand, product, or service being talked about is part of a buzz marketing campaign. Thus, you'll want to instigate institutional word of mouth for your store as a way to spur everyday word of mouth among your customers.

What's the Buzz? Buzz marketing has been not as clearly defined as word-of-mouth marketing. For example, *Newsweek* magazine defined buzz as "infectious chatter; genuine, street-level excitement about a hot new person, place or thing" and interpreted buzz marketing as marketing associated with fads or trends that are popular for a brief period.[6] So what is the bottom line? Importantly, it is that word of mouth can be institutionally developed. If someone can do it on a broad national scale, you can do it in your store on a much smaller and controllable scale with your customers. That is, as long as you understand and implement the practices correctly.

Why not hire a company to develop your word-of-mouth marketing for you? Why not hire actors? Because you need to understand your customer. *You* need to talk to them—you yourself—not some company. You want to be hands-on, not hands-off. And only by creating and working on these programs with your employees can you do that. Simply put, you understand your business better than anyone, and you are in the best position to share information about your store with your customers. The customer becomes interested in you. They have a positive experience. They pass it on. It is that simple.

The Viral Difference. Viral marketing is somewhat like word-of-mouth marketing in that it uses the power of preexisting social networks such as those that exist on the Internet to promote products or services. In general, viral marketing refers to specific tactics on the Internet, such as placing a video on a service like YouTube.

Viral marketing relies on an individual seeing a message (such as a video) and then alerting friends and family online about his or her discovery. In turn, these individuals alert more friends and family about the message. Additionally, viral marketing is often seen as stealth marketing, since the identity of the sponsor is rarely known. Part of the value of such stealth campaigns is that people spend time trying to find out the sponsor's identity, and the discovery of the identity leads to even more communication. Part of the viral nature of the marketing efforts comes from the search of the discovery of who the marketer is. A great example of this is a recent viral video that showed an interview with a gentleman who made a robot out of a Mini Cooper. The video's URL was circulated widely around the Internet, with many viewers wondering who made the video. After it had been out several weeks, viewers discovered it was a video created by Mini Cooper's ad agency, Crispin Porter and Bogusky.

Don't Be Shilly! Shill marketing is a type of word-of-mouth marketing in which marketers hire actors to spread the word about your store to other people. The scooter maker Vespa, for example, hired models to drive Vespas to popular night spots and tell patrons about the Vespa. This type of marketing is seen by many consumers as unethical, since the identity of the person sharing the comments is hidden. We will talk more about the ethics of this in Chapter 8.

GETTING STARTED: UNDERSTANDING THE IMPACT OF WORD OF MOUTH

In the early days of communication research, a theory called one-step flow suggested that all messages were magic bullets that went directly from senders to receivers, and all audiences processed all messages in the exact same way. This theory was replaced by a theory known as the two-step flow, which said that messages were not magic bullets. Instead, a message influenced a small number of individuals who then influenced their peers through word of mouth.[7] The researchers termed these influential individuals opinion leaders, and these people became the original sources of word of mouth.

Even before the Internet became so popular, researchers were busy examining how word of mouth was different from other forms of messages. In 1955, for example, two researchers investigating factors influencing consumer brand switching found that word of mouth was seven times more effective than newspaper and magazine advertising and more than twice as effective as radio ads. This study, conducted in the fledgling days of television, did not even consider that medium. In 1971, another researcher found that WOM was nine times more effective than any type of advertising in changing negative or neutral attitudes about a brand to positive attitudes.

Much of the more recent work has examined negative word of mouth. A recent study done at Wharton Business School found that out of 100 people who have a bad experience at your store, about a third will no longer come to your store. But out of those 100 people, only 6 will tell you about the bad experience. As we have talked about in the last chapter, you need to use customer research to be vigilant about noting whether your customers have positive experiences.

But there is more to the study. Only six customers will tell you about the bad experience. However, thirty-one will tell their friends and family about the bad experience. Yes, they will be spreading negative word of mouth about your store, and you probably do not even know that they had a bad experience! And what's more, most of those people will tell two or more people.[8] If that does not convince you to monitor satisfaction with your place of business, we do not know what would!

As we have said before, we recommend that you use your current customers to talk about your store, or to put it another way, to become champions for you. These people, especially the Family and the Flirts, know and appreciate your store. Additionally, you will want to manage what your customers tell others to make sure that they are talking about the important things that others will care about. Earlier we referred to these important things as *comments*; the Word of Mouth Marketing Association calls them *episodes*. Next, we'll look at how and when these comments and episodes occur.

MOVING FORWARD: THE ELEMENTS OF A WORD-OF-MOUTH CAMPAIGN

WOMMA defines a word-of-mouth episode as a single occurrence of word-of-mouth communication.[9] The process of a word-of-mouth episode (as outlined by WOMMA) involves five unique elements:

- The Word-of-Mouth Unit: *The content of the word-of-mouth message.*
- The Participants: *The first people to share the information with each other.*
- The Venues: *Where they are likely to talk about it.*
- The Actions: *What do we expect them to do.*
- The Outcomes: *What results are likely to occur.*

We will go over each of these concepts and provide examples to help you understand each of them. Then we will follow that up with a real-life example of decision making regarding word of mouth.

The Word-of-Mouth Unit, Also Known as the "What"

The Word of Mouth Marketing Association defines this as a single unit of marketing-relevant information shared by a customer. Several qualities make up an optimal word-of-mouth unit. It is topical, meaning that that information about your store is the focus of the conversation. It is timely in that it reflects a product, service, or activity that is currently available at your store. It is positive in that the key customer talking about your store is saying good things about your store to others. It is clear in that it is easy to understand, and it is persuasive in that the person hearing the message will want to take action on the message.

Note that we called that the *optimal* message. One of the challenges with word of mouth is that you, as the creator of the message, will be able to control the message only up to a point. You may develop an optimal message with all the characteristics noted above, but once your customers start talking, you will no longer have control. So developing optimal messages that will be easy for your customers to communicate is essential.

The Participants, Also Known as the "Who"

Participants are the individuals whose actions make up a word-of-mouth episode. There are three different participants: the creator, the sender, and the receiver.

The creator is the person who creates a word-of-mouth unit. In your store, this could be one of your employees, or you when you contact customers by phone. Anybody who interacts with the customer can create a word-of-mouth unit or experience.

The sender is the person who distributes a WOM unit. This is the person who was so happy about the experience in your store that they could not wait to tell someone about it.

The receiver is the person who receives the WOM unit. This one is easier. This is the person that hears the word-of-mouth message from the sender.

Participants can fill several roles. You will act as a creator, but you do not have a WOM unit until a sender passes it along. A sender may alter the message, and then they will be considered both a creator and a sender. And if the receiver passes it along, they will become a sender, too.

The Venues, Also Known as the "Where"

The venue is the location where the communication takes place. The venue can be online (such as through an electronic medium) or in a traditional physical location. It can be an event, or it can be a piece of physical mail. Understanding the venue is important since you can have a better perception of the total possible audience for the WOM unit, the actual audience who receives the WOM unit. Understanding the venue will also help you understand whether there are any specific rules or standards that may affect the word-of-mouth message.

For example, your customers may be happy to talk to you about your store while they are in your store, but they will not want to talk to you if they run into you at a soccer game. However, they will talk to friends about their shopping experience at a soccer game. Experience is often the best way to understand the best conversations for different venues.

The Actions, Also Known as the "How"

Actions are the specific things that participants do to create, pass along, or respond to a WOM message. Basically, it is the action of a sender telling a receiver about your store. It may be through telling them in person at that soccer game, it may be through an email. Some of this might happen naturally, but other actions will be precipitated by your encouragement. For example, you might want to specifically ask shoppers to tell their friends about the information you share with them.

The Outcomes, or the "Why"

This is the actual marketing impact of the word-of-mouth episode. Many things can happen when someone receives a word-of-mouth message. In many cases, the receiver does nothing with it. Other times, receivers will seek more information about the message to confirm that it is true. There may be a conversion: that is, the receiver will visit your store. The receiver can redistribute the original message, or create a message of his or her own. What does this mean for you? The key to measuring or seeing if your efforts at word of mouth are working is to see if the new guest service you implemented, or the new product, or new information you put out to customers is impacting sales of the total store or that item. Remember it might happen fast or it might take weeks. Be patient.

MOVING FORWARD: USING INFORMATION TO CREATE WORD OF MOUTH

Now that you understand all the elements that go into a word-of-mouth marketing campaign, it is time to put it all together and start the process. In Chapter 2, you learned the importance of that initial conversation with your customers in order to collect data about them. Now is the time to use that information to continue the conversation. Your research should indicate what types of things are of interest to your customers. You are ready to continue sharing information with them, with the goal of soliciting even more feedback from them. So you know the participants, and now it is time to figure out the rest of your program.

Identify the Word-of-Mouth Unit

What do you say in these communications? Your research will tell you what customers like and dislike about your store. Reinforce the things they like and talk about how you are changing the things they do not like (if you can). Your messages can be a mix of information about your store in general, information

WOM in Action. An independent yarn store, which we will call YarnTique, has a unique mix of products and services. In a market with four other yarn stores, YarnTique offers several products that are not available anywhere else. They offer locally produced, one-of-a-kind yarn from nearby farms, as well as numerous brands of high-end yarn for knitting socks. They also offer personal advice and instruction for anyone who buys yarn at their location.

- The word-of-mouth unit: YarnTique has one-of-a-kind yarn and personal instruction to help you create unique projects.
- The participants:
  - The creators: salespeople, who pass on samples of unique yarn to all customers.
  - The senders: loyal customers of YarnTique.
  - The receivers: other knitters who may not be loyal customers.
- The venues: at knitting circles and other activities where knitters meet.
- The actions: showing their knitting friends the sample yarn.
- The outcomes: several new customers visit YarnTique. It is hoped that over a one-month period, five new customers will buy the one-of-a-kind yarn, and existing customers will become even more loyal.

on products or services that might be of interest to your consumers, and information on people who work in your store. Remember this is a dialogue with your customer not just a one-way communication, so always think about what you want to hear from them based on what you are giving them. Here are some examples of the types of conversation starters that you can consider.

Information on your store. People like to shop in stores where they feel welcome and where they can get their business done efficiently. Talking about your store will make customers feel at home. Here is some information about your store you will want to pass on:

- **The 411.** Any changes in the store basics, such as opening and closing hours (if, for instance, you have extended hours during the holiday season), if you now take debit and credit cards, or if you have added a drive-through window. All these things are news about the store that people will be interested in. You can also ask them about changes you're considering to see what their feedback might be.
- **Service enhancements.** Promote any new services that your store offers, such as gift wrapping, mailing, or repairs. If you run a restaurant, you can query your customers about menu additions you are considering. If this service is only offered seasonally, indicate that also.
- **Community events.** Are the Girl Scouts selling cookies in front of your store this weekend? Will the Bloodmobile be parked nearby? If so, let your customers know. You probably offer to put up posters for the local high

school play or for an upcoming concert or dance event. Why not give that event a little mention to your customers? It is a great way to show support for your community and to become an information resource for customers on things beyond the purpose of your store.

- **Community groups.** Here you're doing more than just supporting a particular event—you're helping a group raise money. This effort builds WOM with the members of the group, plus it builds goodwill with your other customers. When you alert them to your support of a particular group, you can ask them for suggestions of other, affiliated organizations to support.
- **Sneak peek on store-wide promotions.** Give customers advance notice of sales and other events to make them feel in the know. This will also encourage them to plan to stop at your store during the event. As part of your dialogue, you can ask them what kind of customer-only specials they might like to see.
- **Cross-promotions with other stores.** Share information about the retail area in which your store is located. Upcoming sidewalk sales, flower shows, and other shopping-district events will be of interest to many different customers. You can even post a calendar of events for the upcoming month or couple of months and ask them for suggestions of other retailers they think you should partner with where they think the service and quality match up with your store.
- **Loyalty and reward program information.** In the next chapter, we will discuss loyalty and reward programs to keep your customers coming back to the store. If you are just starting a program, or if you are making changes to the program, take the opportunity to tell your customers. As you will see in the next chapter, it is very important to solicit their feedback on loyalty efforts.
- **Contests or sweepstakes.** If your store will be sponsoring a contest or sweepstakes drawing, describe the rules and procedures to your customers. You can encourage participation by saying something like this: "For our annual holiday promotion we are considering the following prizes. Which one do you think works the best?"
- **Gift ideas for upcoming holidays.** Tell your customers about interesting and unique gift ideas that they might not have thought about. Also be sure to tell them where in the store the gifts are located.
- **Service and staff improvements.** Tell your customers what type of training sessions or staff improvements you are doing. Customers are always interested in hearing what you are doing to help improve the staff. It makes them feel good that you are trying to develop your people. For instance, "Our chef is going to be gone for a week on vacation in Italy but promises to come back with some new recipes that he learned while there."

Information on products and services. Many customers have selected your store because of the specific products and services you offer. If you talk to them about your products and services, you are on your way to getting them to tell others.

New product lines. It is likely that you are always adding new products or services to your product mix, so this could be a rich area of information to explore. What exactly does new mean?

If your store is a	*New can mean . . .*
Restaurant	Items added to the menu
Salon or spa	Treatments that you now provide, or changes you have made to existing treatments
Apparel or shoe store	Lines that you carry that you have not carried before
Jewelry store	Up-and-coming designers
Coffee shop	Different flavors, concoctions new to your location

- **Seasonal product lines.** Let your customers know when you have Christmas cards in stock, or when the freshest fish is available.
- **Upgrades to products.** Does one of your popular product lines have new formulations or features? Providing the information to your customers lets them increase their product knowledge.
- **Customer favorites.** What if you talked about the favorite purchases of some of your Family to your other customers? For example, talk about the retirees who meet for pastries once a week, the husband who picks up some chocolates for his wife once a month, the kids stocking up for back to school. These human interest stories are a great way to give your store a unique personality.
- **In-store events.** If you are going to be demonstrating a new product or offering a sample of a new food line, let people know the details.
- **Promotions and sales.** Provide information when specific products or services go on sale.

Information on employees. Personal connection with people in the store is powerful to creating relationships and generating WOM. You need to make it optional for your staff. Some employees are excited about what is happening in their lives, while others want to keep details private. Once the staff sees that most of the comments from customers are extremely positive, more of them will feel comfortable about sharing personal information.

- **Staff bios.** Ask staff members to write a paragraph describing their background, their families, their hobbies and outside interests, and why they like working in your store. This gives customers a better feeling about your employees and may even start conversations between employees and customers ("Didn't I see your picture . . . ?"). Examples that work include birthdays, marriages, births, grandkids, graduations, hobbies, vacations, and the like. You need to stay away from negative stories about divorces and disease; keep it related to the store as much as possible. Let the staff person decide what to share.

- **New hires with their expertise.** Does your new bartender come from one of the hottest restaurants? Has the new salesperson at your outdoor store climbed Mount Rainier? Announce your new hires with fanfare!
- **Customer service stories.** Did someone write a letter saying something good (or even something bad) about your store? You should always answer the letter with another letter either thanking them for the nice words or apologizing for any problems and providing information about how you are going to correct any issues. Ask the letter writer if you can share the letter. If the person obliges, share it with others and include your response. Look what you've done: You have started a conversation with one person and used that to start more conversations with others. This is WOM in spades. It is what WOM is all about. You honor the person who told you the service story, and you encourage others to pass on the story. This in turn reminds them of similar experiences they have had.

> **Action Idea:** Select four of the types of information just described, and create a communication around each one. Review your current marketing plan (which you started based on the information you learned in Chapter 1) and evaluate whether any of the information items in this section relate to a certain promotion that you already have planned. For example, if you are planning out January and February, think about sending a message about Valentine's Day products toward the end of January. Put these word-of-mouth units in the marketing plan/grid that you started as part of Chapter 1.

MOVING FORWARD: DELIVERING THE COMMUNICATION

Once you have determined what you are going to say and to whom you are going to say it, you can consider how you will get the information to them.

Identify the Venues

The first step is to determine whether you will use offline or online techniques or both. This decision will depend in part on your budget and in part on the amount of time and technical expertise that you have. Email and other online techniques are the most efficient ways to reach large groups of people. In-store techniques are more personal. Many people love to get paper mail. You really cannot go wrong with what you select. Select more than one contact point and use different contact mechanisms every month to keep your messages fresh.

> **Action Idea:** Select one or two venues for your first word-of-mouth effort. Note when you will start these activities to your marketing grid.

Next, you should determine how often you should talk to your customers. It is a bit of a balancing act: You need to have something to tell them so they do not think you are wasting their time, and you need to keep talking to them regularly. The key is relevant, meaningful conversation. With that in mind, you could speak or connect with your customers every week or every month with something new. It could also depend on the frequency of purchase. If your customers are coming to your store weekly or even daily, it makes sense to interact or connect more frequently. Less frequent purchase cycles would mean you should be careful not to overwhelm your customers with too much in an attempt to get them in. Remember, you want a long-term relationship with your customers, not just a short-term bump in business. And of course, you should always give your customers the option of opting out of your communications if they no longer wish to converse with you.

> **Action Idea:** Refer to your marketing grid and schedule word-of-mouth efforts based on how frequently customers visit your store.

Identify the Actions

Now that you know whom you are talking to, what you're saying, and through what channel, all you have to do is identify the specific actions that you expect to occur for each word-of-mouth event. For example, say you plan to talk to your customers in store, via a newsletter, and through targeted email. Which messages will be used in which venues? What exactly do you want customers to do with that information? Here are some ideas.

In-store techniques

- **Management by walking around.** Spend some time or so every day walking around the store and talking to your customers. Select one of your conversation starters to use as the first thing you say to the person, and use the opportunity to ask the shopper what he or she thinks and feels about your store. At first, you may need to explain what you are doing so shoppers do not feel hassled by your presence ("We are spending some time this month chatting with our customers about our store"). Do this for five minutes a couple of times a day, and not always at the same time. Walk around and interact with your guests at different times, maybe for just five or ten minutes five or six times a day. In this way, it will not seem programmed but very real. It will also give you a good idea of what happens at different times of the day. Plus, you meet new people that you have not met before, and this will make them feel special. Leverage this good feeling and ask them to tell their friends about their visit.

- **Chatting at an in-store event.** On those occasions you have a product demo or a sampling, spend some time having casual conversations with your guests. Ask them what other types of in-store events they would be interested in. Encourage them to get back to you if they have other ideas.
- **Salespeople's "question of the day."** You can encourage your salespeople to start conversations with your customers by providing them with a question of the day. Some stores instruct their employees to ask something like, "Did you find everything you need?" at checkout. While this is a fine question, it is a yes/no question, and does not allow the conversation to flow. Focus on a single question to make capturing the information easier for the staff and for you to understand what the customers are saying. If the customer indicates that they would like to chat a bit about the store, encourage your salespeople to do so and to use that conversation to give out more information about the store. Encourage salespeople to ask customers to tell their friends.
- **Store newsletter.** Develop a quarterly store newsletter that can be available at the store or mailed out. It does not have to be long, detailed, or glossy, but it does need to contain information that your customers will be interested in. Keep the newsletter short, punchy, and easy to read. Doing so will make it easier to write and keep doing. You also need to be sure to include contact information so you can begin a dialogue with customers. You might even offer a coupon that customers could bring in that includes a question or two to find out how your store is doing in their eyes. Have a mailing list sign-up at the cash register to collect names and either postal or email addresses.
- **Suggestion box/board.** Have a printed card that says something like, "Give us feedback!" or "Talk to us" available at the checkout or at a counter or table in your store. Have a supply of pens and a box where your customers can place their suggestions. Every so often, answer customer questions or comments and place them on a bulletin board or in your newsletter so other customers will see how you respond to customer comments. People want to know that they are being listened to, so anything you can do to indicate that their comments are important will help keep the dialogue going.

Action Idea: Think about which of these in-store techniques you have both the time and the physical space for. Select one or two to try for a few months, and see if you are getting the information you need to make good decisions and keep conversations going. Make note of the activity on your marketing grid.

Online techniques

Does your store have a Web site? Many stores have an Internet presence where they sell items online, but many have a presence without becoming involved in e-retailing. Developing a Web site is worth considering. Many consumers now research choices on the Internet, even if they make the purchase in the actual store. You can show your hours, the different product categories you offer, links to suppliers, and contact information. It does not have to have many bells and whistles (though of course, it can!), and can be set up fairly quickly using a simple software program. When you sign up with an Internet host, you will also get the capability to email your customers with an email address identifying your store and even the purpose of the message (i.e., news@yourstore.com).Visit our Web site for more information about how to get started with your online activities.

Once you have a Web site with an address such as www.yourstore.com, you can provide different contact opportunities for your customers. These include:

- **"Contact us" link.** Whatever you have on your Web page, you should always prominently display your contact us link. This link should either go to a fill-in form that allows customers to share information with you, or to a page where all they have to do is type in their message and it will be sent to you. You should highlight this link whenever possible, and encourage people to use it (by adding words such as "we would love to hear from you").
- **Email alerts.** Email alerts should contain one or two pieces of information each week. They should be brief, and should end with an invitation for the readers to let you know their thoughts on that week's news. While not every recipient will respond, the responses you do get will tell you whether the information is seen positively or negatively. You can keep track of those responses to monitor which types of information appear to be most useful to your customers. Additionally, you can respond to each response with a thank-you and a reminder to the customers to continue to let you know what they like and do not like.

    Have different ways for customers to sign up for the email alerts. Have an email sign up sheet at the register, or collect email addresses on customer surveys to start to build a customer database. You will also want to see if your point of sale system allows you to collect this information when your customer checks out. And have a place on your Web site where people can sign up for email alerts. Whenever you collect this information, though, be sure to ask your customer's permission to send them emails. If they say yes, you are on your way! However, you should always give customers instructions on how to stop receiving emails if they do not want them any longer. By following these guidelines, you will avoid being seen as a spammer by your customers.

- **Email newsletter.** If you publish a newsletter that you distribute in the store, you might also want to think about producing it electronically (one way is to save it as a PDF file). You can either email it to your customers and/or have it available for download on your Web site. The costs for the electronic version will be much lower than the costs of printing (and especially mailing), so you will want to encourage shoppers to use this method whenever possible. You will also have that information available to people who were not in the store when the newsletter was issued. This ensures that you will be in touch with your customers regardless of how often they visit, and this is always a bonus.

Action Idea: Select which of the techniques above you are most comfortable starting, and sit down with the calendar for the next two months. You will see when you have certain things planned, and now you can think about when you want to send out information on activities or anything else.

Whether offline or online, remember: The purpose of all these activities is not to have a one-way flow of information from you to your customer, it is to encourage a continual dialogue between you and your customers. Whatever channels and methods you suggest, you should always encourage your customers to contact you about the information. Always take advantage of your message to alert customers to anything of interest. If you are sending out a new service alert, for instance, provide a link or cross-reference to the specials section to tell them there is a special on as well. It reminds them constantly about the other sections of information at their disposal.

Here is a quick guide to how initiate a dialogue.

If you are using . . .	*Then remember to . . .*
Management by walking around	—Ask your customers what other events they would like to see in-store.
	—Encourage them to let you know if they have questions or comments.
	—Pass out cards with your contact information for them to fill out and drop in the suggestions box.
Salespeople question of the day	—Have your salespeople track responses.
	—Ask your salespeople to tell you their top line summary of what they have heard.
	—Remind salespeople to give customers contact information if they ask for it.

	—Follow up via your regular contact if you make any changes.
	—Change the question regularly.
Store newsletter	—Signal via words and graphics that you are interested in hearing from customers.
	—Remember to provide contact information: a name, email address, and phone number.
	—Follow up on every contact.
Suggestion box/board	—Respond to comments.
	—Communicate changes that you make based on the comments.
Web page contact us link	—Signal via words and graphics that it is easy to contact you.
	—Respond to every person who replies.
Email alerts	—Encourage response by adding a line that says "let me know what you think!"
Email newsletter	—Do not just send out the email with the newsletter as an attachment; thank people for taking the time to email you and encourage them to send you questions and comments.

The thread for all of these is that you need to encourage people to contact you and then you need to respond—fairly quickly—when they do. Try to respond to emails within twenty-four hours or written comments within a week. This will reinforce your interest in them and their thoughts and it should help them develop strong feelings about your store.

Set aside time each day as your contact time—time to be in contact with your customers via the Internet and in your store. It is the most important investment of your entire marketing program.

Regardless of whether you are responding in person or in writing, practice active listening. Ask the customer for more information or clarification on any of their comments that you do not quite understand. Try to get to the heart of any problem, and try to find out the source of any great customer experiences. Both of these will help you get the fullest picture of what is happening at your store, and will help your customers feel that their opinion really counts.

Identify the Outcomes

Setting goals and measuring how you're achieving those goals is an important barometer of the success of your word-of-mouth marketing plan. We go over measurement in great detail in Chapter 8. However, another important outcome is that the word of mouth changes from institutional to everyday.

Action Idea: Continue the conversation. As part of your ongoing conversations, encourage your customers to start spreading the word. This involves creating opportunities for conversations beyond the formal collection of customer data. It starts with announcing changes that you have made based on customer input. As the dialogue gets rolling, you will discover more things to do in your store, which will result in more things to talk about.

Whatever you do, be sure to make it easy to get back to you with their thoughts and comments, so the conversation is not just a one-way communication. And remember, anytime you collect personal information (such as an email or postal address) from a customer, tell them that the information will not be shared without their permission.

TAKING IT FURTHER: WORKING WITH TRADITIONAL ADVERTISING

Traditional advertising can help strengthen and build your customer community. It can reinforce all the positive feelings that your customers have about you. It validates their decisions to use your store. "That is a great ad for O'Leary's. I really like that place." Or it can cause customers to start WOM all over again. "That ad for O'Leary's reminds me of the last time that I was there, and they made my day with the service I received."

Make sure to use advertising to reinforce what you are doing with your direct communications to your customers. The advertising can remind them about the alert that you sent (or maybe the alert reminded them of the ad they saw). Added exposure should result in added business.

Word of mouth complements traditional advertising through credibility and frequency. At a minimum, word of mouth will increase the frequency that someone sees or hears a message. Since word-of-mouth messages are seen as more credible than traditional advertising messages, they may have more impact on the people who hear them. In this way, a WOM message will confirm what someone hears or sees in traditional media or will add more information and relevance to a traditional advertisement.

The integration of traditional advertising and word of mouth also creates recency. *Recency* is the ability of the message to reach someone close to a purchase decision. Consumers often ask friends and families for recommendations shortly before they go shopping. If one of these shoppers asks one of your customers about a product available at your store, and if your customer has recently received some new information from you about your store, your customer is likely to share that information with that shopper. Recency, then, is a strategic determination of when you should share information with your customers.

TAKING IT FURTHER: USING WORD OF MOUTH WITH THE FAMILY, FLIRTS, AND PHANTOMS

In your customer research, you've learned about some of the key differences between your store's Family, Flirts, and Phantoms. The next step is to begin word-of-mouth programs targeted specifically for them. The way to start is to first figure out what information your customers will be most interested in matched to the information you have to tell them. You should probably have a mix of a couple different types of information to appeal to the different segments.

- The Family is probably very familiar with your store and its offerings, so they will want the sneak peek information as well as information about the people that they see when they visit your store (i.e., your employees and other customers).
- The Flirts and Phantoms will want more reasons to visit your store, so talking about the in-store events and upcoming promotions will be of interest to them. These two groups will probably enjoy a coupon, too. Try a value-added offer that combines multiple discounts or multiple services so that the offer is unique and stands out relative to the competition. Mailing to new customers is key.

Then consider how you will start the conversations. What specific venues will work with all these groups? We suggest using both a written method and a face-to-face method to start with, like combining management by walking around with a newsletter or email alert. Multiple channels help encourage conversations since people will be able to respond in the manner in which they are most comfortable. As you get proficient with the two methods, add a third. The goal is to be conversing with as many customers as possible. Your optimal number of methods will depend on when you are reaching all your customers who are open to communicating with you.

We have given you many ideas of what to say, and where and how to say things. In a perfect world, your customers will be so excited about learning this information that they will rush right out to tell their friends. However, it is not a perfect world, and not everyone who learns something about your store is going to talk about it to his or her friends. So you need to focus on creating a core group who will be most likely to be part of the word-of-mouth process. At this point, we would like you to consider the types of people who are most likely to become customer evangelists.

TAKING IT FURTHER: CREATING AND WORKING WITH STORE CHAMPIONS

Word of mouth is going to build some serious Champions for your store. While it is important to talk to all your customers, it is also important for you to remember that not all customers are going to become Champions for your store. The ones who are likely to talk about your store have been termed (by various authors) the magic people, the trendsetters, the influencers, the mavens and the ravens, the evangelists, the connectors, and the advocates. And do not forget our term from earlier this chapter, the opinion leaders. Whatever you call them, they are your Store Champions and they are important.

Who are they? They are the people who not only spread the word about your company to others but can help you recruit new customers and improve your products and services. They will be your staunch defenders and supporters.

They are enthusiastic consumers. They like to shop, and they like to make recommendations about stores and brands. However, they are not necessarily brand loyal. Because they are enthusiastic, they are willing to try new things. So do not think just because someone is part of your Family that he or she will be a good individual to encourage to generate word of mouth about your store. The Flirts and the Phantoms are just as likely to be Store Champions.

Store Champions are seen by other people as credible sources of information. This credibility can be developed in several different ways. Store Champions can be seen as highly knowledgeable with expertise in a specific category due to their job or their avocation. For example, you might have a friend or relative who works with computers, and you contact him or her anytime you have a question about your own computer, including purchasing software and peripherals. Your sister who has four dogs might be your best source for information about local pet stores and vets, but not about your computer.

Store Champions are also seen as credible because they have researched various categories, and they might be able to give advice on selection criteria or reliable information sources. Their knowledge of the category goes much farther than recommending a single brand. They will be able to tell why they recommend it. For example, car enthusiasts know a lot about a number of car models, not just the one they drive. Fashion enthusiasts read all the monthly fashion magazines like *Vogue* and *Elle*.

The best enthusiasts have large social networks—groups of people with whom they interact on a regular basis. This is because you do not want people who are enthusiasts in a single category only talking to other enthusiasts; it probably will not affect your market. You want them talking to people who may or may not talk about products or services very often. Research shows that people pass along information to friends and family members most often, but also to people who share the same interests, work colleagues, neighbors, community group members, and fellow parents at kids activities.[10]

SUMMING UP

In this chapter, we have shown you:

- What exactly word of mouth, buzz marketing, viral marketing, and shill marketing are.
- How word of mouth is an effective complement to traditional advertising.
- The word-of-mouth process, and the different types of decisions you need to make to begin your word-of-mouth campaign.
- The differences in how word of mouth can work for Family, Flirts, and Phantoms.
- The importance of having Store Champions, and how to identify and utilize these important people.

What motivates people to talk about your store? What do they get out of it? For most people, their enthusiasm for buying things spills over into their enthusiasm for being part of a large, chatty social network. For some, they get to be an opinion or information leader among their social network. They like to be the person that others look to for trends, new ideas, and the latest thing. For others, they get the feeling that they are an insider and know about things before anyone else does. Others are motivated by altruism: wanting those in their social networks to make smart shopping decisions (just as they do!). Assessing and rewarding these motivations is what the next chapter is all about.

RESOURCE TOOLBOX

Our Web site (www.underdognetwork.com) has links to lots of online resources, whether you have a site, you need to set up a site, or you need to find a great source to help with your email newsletters. One source for the latter is a company called Constant Contact (www.constantcontact.com). The type of system offered by Constant Contact and other vendors not only allows you to send out your emails, it also provides tracking capabilities so you can find out how people are using your messages. Are they opening them and reading them? Are they sending them along to friends? Being able to track your efforts is a huge strength of the Internet.

Chapter 4

Encouraging and Rewarding Word of Mouth with Family, Flirts, and Phantoms

Customers → *Conversations* → Community → Commitment

You have started the conversation with your customers, and now it is time to encourage them to talk to others in their social network about your store. In the Getting Started section we will discuss how to ask people to tell others about your store. In the Moving Forward section, we will show you how to thank people for telling others about your store. In the Taking It Further sections we will talk about refinements to such programs.

Ask your customers to tell others. And thank them when they do. That is this chapter in a nutshell.

GETTING STARTED: ASKING YOUR CUSTOMERS TO TALK ABOUT YOUR STORE

The simple idea of asking your customers to tell others about your store is basic, yet many store owners never think to do it. We learned earlier that conversations about products and services are a natural part of people's everyday conversations. Remember the research that found that eight conversations each day focus on brands? Knowing this, you might think that your customers will be ready and able to talk about your store to their friends, families, and colleagues without any encouragement from you. In some cases, this will be true. But for most people, messages and knowledge about your store shares their mind space with information about all the other products and services they use on a daily basis, plus all the other information that we need to get through the day: where the car keys are, what time soccer practice is over, and so on. Additionally, some people will assume that if you are not asking for more customers, you might not need any.

Therefore, you will want to ask your customers to tell their friends. Not in a pushy, aggressive way, but in a consistent way so they will be able to bring up your store when the time is right. You are already communicating regularly with many of your customers, and you can use these channels to ask and remind them to tell those in their social network about your store.

At this point, let's review the different channels so we can show you how to encourage people to spread the word. Table 4-1 describes the different communication channels that we talked about in Chapter 3, and we have added some simple hints on how you can ask your customers to tell others for each channel.

Many of the methods that we described in the table allow you to pinpoint not only who is talking about your store, but whom they are talking to. This is important information to know for several reasons. You can track how effective your word-of-mouth efforts are by seeing how many of your customers are passing along the messages that you want them to. If you are using multiple channels, you can start to identify which channels are most effective for word of mouth. And once you start providing rewards to your customers, you can see how those rewards affect word-of-mouth messages. Additionally, once you get new customers to your store based on these messages, you can start the dialogue process with them and hopefully convert them to word-of-mouth key customers for your store.

MOVING FORWARD: UNDERSTANDING REWARD AND LOYALTY SYSTEMS

As we mentioned in Chapter 3, at some point along the word-of-mouth process you will begin to lose control of the message. And that point is now: when you ask your key customers to talk about your store to other people. From this point on you cannot control what your customers will say. What you can do is make sure that they have the tools and the knowledge to be the best ambassadors for your store that they can be.

Also, keep in mind that when you can ask your best customers to become Store Champions for you, one of two things can happen. Either the customer will start to talk about your store to others, or she will not. On top of that, either your customer will help you track her communications or others, or she will not. For these reasons, it is important to have continual communications with all your customers, and even more important, to find ways to reward them for patronage and, hopefully, for their participation as key customers.

Thanking Customers

Everyone likes to be thanked. Everyone likes their work and their ideas to be acknowledged. There are many different ways that you can thank your customers, some directly linked to referring others to your store, some thanking them for their continued business. They all can have a place in your store, and they can all have some type of impact on your word-of-mouth plans. They have their

Table 4-1 Encouraging Customers to Spread the Word

If you are using	And you are	Then you can also
Management by walking around	Asking customers what other events they'd like to see in store	Ask them to bring their friends to future events
	Encouraging them to let you know if they have questions or comments	Remind them that you are open to ideas not only from them but also from their friends and family
	Passing out cards with your contact information or for them to fill out and drop in the suggestions box	Give them extra cards for their friends and family
Salespeople question of the day	Having your salespeople track responses	Have salespeople track how customers heard about your store (this will start to measure word of mouth); if customers name a friend who told them, take note of that person's name
	Asking your salespeople to tell you their top line summary of what they have heard	Have salespeople ask if they tell friends about what they have bought
	Changing the question regularly	Have salespeople remind them to tell friends about the sale going on
	Reminding salespeople to give customers contact information if they ask for it	Give salespeople cards or coupons to give to customers for their friends
	Following up via your regular contact if you make any changes	

strengths and weaknesses, and they can be tweaked to appeal to the Family, the Flirts, and the Phantoms. We will discuss three major types of programs in this chapter: reward programs, loyalty programs, and referral programs. You may choose to implement one, two, or all three of these programs, depending on your customers and your goals.

Reward Programs

You may hear the terms reward program and loyalty program used interchangeably. And that is logical, since it makes perfect sense to think that if you reward a customer for coming to your store, they are likely to become loyal to your store. There is a specific difference, though, and that has as much to do with your ability to communicate with customers than what your customers get. A *reward program* is designed to create an incentive for a specific activity. These programs generate minimal information about customers as part of the program. A *loyalty program*, on the other hand, allows you to collect information about your customers as part of the rewards.

It is also likely that you and others in your family belong to several reward or loyalty programs at other retailers. These programs have been very popular since 1981, when American Airlines started the first frequent flyer program, which rewarded customers for flying with the airline. As soon as American Airlines introduced its program, other airlines followed. Hotel and rental car company programs joined the airline programs, all hoping to generate more revenue from business travelers. Interestingly, several airlines and rental car companies did not jump on the frequent traveler bandwagon, as they were not convinced that such programs would be effective marketing tools.[1] Specifically, these companies believed that these awards programs would be short-term marketing gimmicks that would quickly disappear. Additionally, some higher-end companies were concerned that a frequent flyer program would be perceived as some type of rebate or discount, which could be seen as inconsistent with a high-end or premium service business. The companies were also concerned about the out-of-pocket costs of the programs.

All of these are valid concerns, and ones that you have probably thought of when contemplating setting up a program. The hotels and rental car companies that delayed setting up the programs found that they underestimated the power of these reward programs, and they suffered market share losses. Today, these types of programs have become part of the "core product" offered by airlines.

Today, almost 30 percent of all Americans belong to some type of credit card reward program, and 24 percent belong to an airline program. About 13 percent of Americans are part of a retail store reward program, with 12 percent involved in restaurant programs. Almost three-fourths of Americans with household incomes over $75,000 participate in at least one reward program, and the vast majority of these individuals say that their membership influences their purchasing decisions.

However, you should also know that there's turnover in these types of programs: About 42 percent of individuals who participate in rewards programs say they have stopped participating in at least one program, and three-fourths of those people say they purchase less from the company after they stopped participating.[2] What does this mean? It is wrong to think a program can be successful without some tender loving care. You need to remind your customers about the program, and keep it fresh and interesting for them. We will give you some ideas on how to do that in a few pages.

MOVING FORWARD: TYPES OF REWARD PROGRAMS

Reward programs are based on a simple idea of positive reinforcement: If you reward someone when she does something that you like, she is likely to do it again. Aaronson developed a typology of awards based on this theory,[3] and he outlined the different types of reward programs as follows:

- *Continuous reinforcement programs* provide some type of reward whenever the customer visits the store.
- *Ratio programs* reward customers based on the number of purchases they make or the amount they spend. With this type of program the reward is either explicit from the start (a fixed ratio, like buy ten, get one free) or the reward is a surprise (a variable ratio, such as a program where you buy a certain number or volume of products, and then scratch off the amount to find out the reward).
- *Interval programs* reward customers at a specified time (a fixed interval, such as senior Tuesday, or a variable interval, where a different reward is given out every hour of a specific day).
- *Token economies*, where one type of metric (such as miles flown) is traded for a product or service (such as a free airline ticket).

Table 4-2 offers more information on these programs.

The similarity among all these programs is that they will all do a good job getting people into your store more frequently. When they come in, you will be able to talk to them and tell them about your store. In addition, while they will not generate a direct referral for your store, these programs give your customers something to talk about to others. The chance that someone will tell others about your store will increase if the customer has a good experience in your store.

Which type of program is right for you? It will depend upon what you want to accomplish first or most in your store. Do not try to have the program that you start out with be the perfect program. You will learn as you go. We have outlined some thoughts about where you might want to start at the end of this chapter.

Aaronson, who developed the typology, has drawn some additional distinctions between the programs. He used three metrics to measure the effectiveness of the reward programs: the learning curve, the frequency, and decay.[4] You can use this information to help you figure out what type of program would be best for you.

Table 4-2 Types of Reward Programs

Type of Reward	Description	Example
Continuous reinforcement	Customer rewarded every time the desired behavior is performed	Free shipping with every order Everyday low price guarantee Premium clubs
Fixed ratio	Customer is rewarded on a fixed schedule: reward given once specific number of purchases is made	Punch card program where once customer has purchased ten cups of coffee he gets one free
Variable ratio	Customer is rewarded on a variable basis; customer will get a reward but does not know what the reward will be	Scratch ticket program where customer gets a discount on a purchase once a certain number of purchases is made; scratchoff box indicates the level of discount
Fixed interval	Customer rewarded based on a specific time interval: such as once per week or once per month	Senior discount days on Tuesdays, teacher discount days once per month
Variable interval	Customer is rewarded on a specific time interval not known to customer	Store offers a different discount every hour of a specific day
Token economy	Points (or some other metric) are accrued and traded for a reward	Frequent flyer programs

The Learning Curve

A learning curve considers how quickly the customer understands the program, and how quickly her behavior will change. It is a measure of how quickly the reward program takes effect.

- *Continuous reinforcement*: These programs have a fast learning curve, which means people learn about these types of program very quickly, and alter their behavior in a fairly short time since the reward is almost instantaneous with the change in behavior.[5] Therefore, these types of programs are great for generating quick initial awareness and sales for your store.
- *Ratio programs* and *token economies*: These programs have a moderate learning curve, which means learning about and earning the reward will take a bit of time.
- *Interval programs:* These programs have a slow learning curve. This means the customer may or may not be able to take advantage of the rewards if he is not in the store when rewards are being offered. These

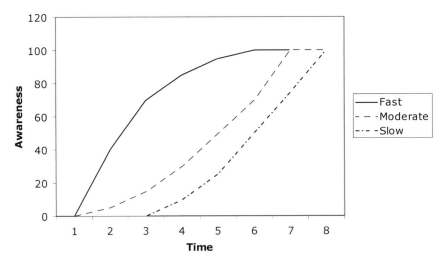

Figure 4-1 Learning Curves

types of programs will need support with traditional advertising to help your customers become aware of them.

Frequency

Frequency shows how often the user interacts with the store when the reward is in place. As we have discussed, the more often someone visits your store, the more opportunities you have to interact with her and the more she will learn about your store to tell to others. In other words, frequency is good. Different types of reward programs will have different effects on shopper frequency. Ratio programs and token economies generate the highest level of frequency, whereas interval programs increase frequency to a lesser extent. However, there is a bit more to it than that. Aaronson factors in whether the frequency is consistent or inconsistent, which helps in your analysis of the different programs.

- *Ratio programs*: With these programs, frequency will increase when customers are close to getting a reward. In our coffee shop example, a customer would buy more frequently when they have seven cups punched on a punch card than two cups. Her shopping frequency is high, but it is inconsistent.
- *Interval programs and token economies*: With these programs, once your customer has learned about them, she will change her behavior to take advantage of the program on the days when it is offered. Customers will visit often to accrue points toward their goal.
- *Continuous reinforcement*: These programs have the least effect on frequency. This could be because shoppers accept these rewards as business as usual at the store, and the rewards do not become special.

Table 4-3 Reward Programs Summary

	Example	Learning Curve	Frequency	Decay
Continuous reinforcement	Free shipping	Very fast	Consistently low	Varies
Fixed ratio	Punch card	Somewhat fast	High but inconsistent	Medium
Variable ratio	Lottery type discount	Fairly slow	High and consistent	Very slow
Fixed interval	Day of week discount	Fairly slow	High and consistent	Very slow
Variable interval	Different product discount every hour	Fairly slow	High and consistent	Very slow
Token economy	Frequent flyer/purchaser	Somewhat fast	High and consistent	Varies

Decay

Decay addresses how the reward affects customer retention. Continuous reinforcement and token economy rewards have the potential of affecting customer retention in a negative way. Here's why: Once the reward is achieved, customers may not wish to continue with the program. However, if the result is something that the customer values, or if the customer's overall loyalty has increased because of the program, the decay may not occur. Decay for these programs is also likely to be a function of whether the customer belongs to similar programs. If you can find a way that she stops using her other programs for yours, decay may not occur. For example, if she turns in her coffee card for a competitive shop to you, give her an extra punch or two on the card for your shop.

Table 4-3 offers a comparison of each of the type of programs.

MOVING FORWARD: SELECTING THE BEST REWARD PROGRAM FOR YOUR BUSINESS

Given this information, how do you select a program? There is no one-size-fits-all answer to this question. Instead, here are some questions to ask about your business to decide which is right for you.

- What is your purchase cycle? Ratio and token economy programs work best with retailers that have a frequent or regular repeat purchase cycle. If someone visits less frequently, an interval program might be a better choice.
- How do customers perceive your store relative to the competition? If customers see little differentiation between you and your competition, a

program that offers a unique reward, using either a continuous reinforcement or ratio program, will increase the frequency in which they visit your store and help create this distinction.

- What type of rewards can you realistically offer? Will the reward be seen as valuable? Put pencil to paper and calculate what type of investment you are considering for your reward program. Offering a reward after twenty cups of coffee will cost less than offering it after ten cups of coffee, but will this be appealing to your customers? Can you afford to offer free shipping with every purchase? Talking to customers about your ideas will help refine your strategy.
- Can you use the program to communicate with customers on an ongoing basis to build relationships? Will this give them something to talk about? One thing to think about is to put a special spin on the program that makes it unique to your store. One yarn store, for example, has a "frequent flyer" program where instead of tracking frequency or dollars spent, they track yards of yarn bought by customers and provide a reward for every mile of yarn bought. This is an interesting twist that can be intriguing to customers and can differentiate the program from others. It also gives customers something interesting to talk about.

Here are some other possible twists.

If your store is a . . .	Try this type of frequency program
Dry cleaner	Track number of sleeves or number of buttons on garments; count extra for garments in a certain color each month (red for February, green for St. Patrick's Day)
Florist	Track number of total flowers purchased (an arrangement might have, for example, twenty or more flowers)
Picture framing store	Track number of total inches of frame purchased
Fast-food restaurant	Track number of French fries or ounces of soda
Fitness trainer	Track the number of inches or pounds of weight loss toward future discounts on sessions
Bookstore	Number of pages purchased

As we discussed in Chapter 3, you have a great opportunity to promote your reward program through the conversations you have with your customers: through newsletters, in-store information, and perhaps even an announcement in traditional advertising vehicles.

TAKING IT FURTHER: CREATING A PERSONALIZED LOYALTY PROGRAM

If you are the only store in town offering a reward program, chances are that you will be quite successful. But how realistic is that? One of the biggest issues with a reward program is that it is something that a competitor can easily copy and even improve on. However, a loyalty program is something different altogether.

Loyalty programs are much less straightforward than reward programs. The reason is simple: As stated earlier in this chapter, loyalty is much more complex than any other feelings or affinities for your store. Loyalty programs are less tangible and more emotional often because they are more personal. They can connect you to your customer on an entirely different level than straight rewards. Therefore, loyalty programs that resonate with customers have less to do with a matrix of tactics and more to do with the depth of knowledge you have about these customers.

The rewards you give to these loyal users should be distinctive from what you provide in the reward program. Regardless of the type of reward, anything that you implement should also allow you to collect more information about your customers. You can then use this information to build a stronger relationship. A strong relationship should also help these loyal customers become strong advocates for your store.

> **Action Idea:** As a first step, think about the people whom you should thank for their loyalty. Consider all the different reasons that people are loyal to your store, and remember loyalty goes beyond what customers spend. Revisit the customer data you collected to think about the different types of loyal customers you have.

Experts agree that a good loyalty program should have three things: a personalized reward, useful information, and one-to-one communication.[6] We will talk about each of these things individually.

Personalized Reward

A personalized reward is a reward that reflects your knowledge of the customer's wants and needs. By *personalized*, we do not mean that every customer has to get a different reward. It means examining what your customers tend to like a lot about your business, and using the reward to get them to know more about what you can do for them. If the reward is in a related category to something she has purchased before, it could work quite effectively. Relevance is the key thought. Is the reward relevant to her? An offer that seems tailor-made just for her will be perceived as recognition of the customer's unique role in your business.

WOM in Action: Hotels seem to really understand the concept of loyalty. Several hotels have loyalty programs that go beyond a punch card or token economy system. Instead, these hotels examine what guests did during their stay, and what they indicated that they liked. This can be done by encouraging reservation and front desk staff to interact with guests and track their preferences. If a guest asked about the location of a local health club on his first visit, the staff should offer passes to a health club or a free massage on his next visit. If a woman customer is traveling alone, she might appreciate an upgrade to the concierge floor on a subsequent visit. Such information could also be collected at a survey done when the customer checks out.

Table 4-4 lists some ideas for loyalty programs.

For some retailers, it will be straightforward to identify the key reason that people are loyal to your store. For many other types of stores, though, you will want to consider looking at different segments of customers and identifying a reward that is more personal to different segments. For some stores, a good way to address loyalty is to allow for customer choice; that is why open-ended gift certificates are often a great way to start these programs. Department stores have been quite effective using these as both an immediate reward as well as a long-term loyalty program.

However, it is also a good idea to use the tracking of purchases to develop your own segments and personal reward programs. The bottom line is that it involves understanding individual preferences, keeping track of them, and then making sure that the preferences are addressed whenever possible.

How can you translate this idea to your store? It will involve some type of tracking of customer purchases, not just in terms of dollar amounts or frequency

Table 4-4 Ideas for Loyalty Programs

If you are a	If your customers	Reward them with
Coffee shop	Buy lots of coffee	A free pastry
Dry cleaners	Bring in lots of sweaters for dry cleaning	A free dry cleaning of their winter coat
Bookstore	Buy books regularly	Invitations to private author events
Camera store	Get photos developed	An enlargement of their favorite photograph in a frame
Shoe store	Buy lots of shoes	Bags to store their shoes in, embroidered with your store's name, or even their own name
Video store	Rent videos frequently	A free bag of microwave popcorn

Table 4-5 Ideas for Developing Your Own Personal Reward Program

If you have a	Look at	Provide rewards
Restaurant	Courses and beverages people buy most often	Reward wine drinkers with discounts on new wine additions; dessert eaters with off-menu desserts
Hardware store	Home vs. garden do it yourselfers (DIYers)	Offer DIYers specials on things they need for a major project; offer gardeners a discount on loam or topsoil
Dry cleaners	Business clothes vs. sports clothes	Offer businesspeople a discount on alterations; arrange a cross-promotion with a sporting goods store for the sports enthusiasts
Clothing store	Business vs. casual clothes	Offer discounts on either a work or play handbag

but also in terms of what specific categories the customer is purchasing. Let us look at some examples so you can see how this might work (see Table 4-5).

You can also use your reward program to keep track of what the members are buying (they must present their card to get the discount) to help you select specific products or services that will be offered at a special price to your best customers. You can alert them to the special via a personal email with a printable coupon that only they can use. Use their purchase data to select new items to add to your product or service mix, and then take the opportunity to personally inform the loyal customer when the new addition is made. Follow up to see if they liked it, and continue to use their information to refine your offerings.

USEFUL INFORMATION

Sometimes a reward is not a discount. Instead, the reward could be useful information that you can share with your loyal customers. This should be proprietary information that others would not have access to. Start by using this information to provide exceptional service to your good customers.

When you read some of these ideas, you might wonder if they might hurt your business. Will customers want to spend money for their favorite dessert at your restaurant if they can make it at home with the recipe you gave them? If they can treat stains themselves, would they not need dry cleaning? You are

WOM in Action: In-N-Out Burger. Something that is not seasonally dependent would be an offer like a secret product or service. An interesting example is In-N-Out Burger's Secret Menu. In-N-Out Burger is a regional chain of restaurants that has several menu items and preparation styles that are not on the published menu but are known by loyal customers. For example, the 3 x 3 burger is a burger (not on the published menu) that comes with three meat patties and three slices of cheese, and you can add meat patties and slices of cheese to make a 4 x 4, 5 x 5, etc. In addition, if you would order your 3 x 3 "Animal Style" you would get a burger with lettuce, tomato, extra spread, pickles, grilled onions, and mustard fried into the patty. The In-N-Out Burger secret menu helps create word of mouth, because the customers wants to tell someone else about what they have learned or created at the restaurant. There are Web sites that In-N-Out users have created on their own to share their passion and secrets for the products at this restaurant.

Action Idea: Use seasonality to reward longevity. One thing many retailers have in common is that you will get in new items or see the nature of your services change with the seasons. For a customer reward, considering offering sneak peeks to the trends for the upcoming seasons, or you can give information on how to prepare for the new season (e.g., prepare your lawn, your car, your clothes).

really creating an even deeper bond of trust and appreciation because the customer now sees you as a trusted friend interested in helping them.

Another twist on the seasonal event would be a customer appreciation night that would feature a speaker or a workshop that is unique to your store. Depending on what your loyal customers are interested in and what your store

Table 4-6 Ideas for Providing Useful Information to Exceptional Customers

If you are a	Provide this type of information	In this type of format
Clothing store	Upcoming fashion trends	Private fashion show
Outdoor store	New products like fishing gear, kayaks, etc.	Test driving event in the store or at a local outdoor venue
Arts and crafts show	When favorite craft items are back in stock	Call customers to tell them
Electronics store	Upgrades to products they have bought in the past	Call or send email to customers to tell them
Restaurant	Secret recipe	Mail or email out to favorite customers
Dry cleaner	Hints and tips on taking care of stains	Produce a brochure or refrigerator magnet and give to customers in the store

sells, you might want to offer, for example, a seminar on cooking, holiday wreath-making, or winterizing your car. Send out invitations or cards inviting loyal customers to the event, and let them know that they will need this special invitation to get in the door after normal business hours (one big box that does a great job of this type of event is the kitchen store Williams-Sonoma). If they cannot attend the event, provide a special discount if they bring the invitation in during normal business hours. You can combine these sneak peeks with a special shopping night where you offer special discounts for that night only. In addition, these events give you an opportunity to invite your customers to bring a friend—another way that positive word of mouth can be developed.

Many of these ideas relate to the broader issue of sharing information about how your business operates or why special services are being added. Say you have just bought a special shipment or got a great deal and you are now passing it on. Even basic information, like the source of goods in your store, can increase the level of interest and involvement. The more you can share, the greater the passion for your store will become and the more word of mouth will be started.

TAKING IT FURTHER: PERSONAL COMMUNICATION AS ITS OWN REWARD

Just as the offer should be personalized, the communication with the customer should be personalized, too. We have already talked about a range of communications that you can have with customers. Keep in mind that you always have opportunities for more personalized communication with the people that you know are your best customers.

If you are inviting a loyal customer to an event, hand-address the postcard invitation and add a handwritten "hope to see you there" to make the invitation more personal. This might seem daunting to do, but your staff can help with this process by addressing the envelopes. This helps them understand their connections to your programs and why they collect the information they do. It also helps their connection to your most loyal customers. They can even say when greeting them, "I sent out your invitation, it is great to see you."

Send each customer a birthday card (if you have that information on file). To stand out, send a card or greeting at an unusual or unexpected time. One realtor, for example, sends out a happy anniversary card to her clients on the anniversary of their house closings. You could also send out a "happy back to school" card to your loyal customers with kids, a happy Arbor Day card to your loyal customers who purchase gardening items, or "happy Indy 500" cards to your auto aficionados. Finally, personalized thank-you notes after the customer has taken advantage of the offer continues the communication and keeps your store top of mind with the customer.

What is next? Once you think you have a good base of loyal customers, we recommend that you then make your loyal customers part of a referral program, which is discussed in the next section.

TAKING IT FURTHER: TURNING LOYALTY INTO REFERRALS

The final type of program we will discuss is a referral program. With a referral program, customers are rewarded specifically for referring others to your store. This is a very specific type of word-of-mouth activity, where you use your key customers to ask someone to shop at your store. Referrals are highly credible. Think about it—when someone you trust tells you about something that they trust, that trust transfers to you.[7] When someone has experienced something firsthand, the referral becomes very powerful.

Referrals are the lifeblood of many businesses. Consumers choose nearly 50 percent of service-providing businesses because of a recommendation.[8] Certain types of service businesses, like insurance agents, chiropractors, auto mechanics, beauty salons, and real estate agents, are particularly reliant on referrals. Referrals are cost-effective, that is, they cost a fraction of what you would pay for a traditional advertising program. Even better, research has shown that people who are referred to a business tend to spend more than those who were not referred. So the cost of acquiring the customer is less, and the income they generate is more.[9]

We have talked at other times in the book about giving people many different and interesting things to talk about your store. While you should definitely keep that up, a referral program tends to be much more specific than the other types of programs we have discussed. You have identified your most loyal customers; you have developed some programs to maintain their loyalty, and now it is the time to ask them specifically to help you by referring your store to their friends and family.

Here is how we recommend that you set up a referral program.

First, decide whom you would like to ask to be what we call your Store Champions, the customers who will be involved in your referral program. You might want to begin with a subset of the Family and Flirts, selecting those individuals who perhaps spend the most money per visit or who visit most frequently. You can introduce the concept of the program with a request to "tell a friend" about the store, or with an invitation to a bring-a-friend special event.

Then, let your best customers know that you are starting a referral program, and that you would like them to be a Store Champion. Some of your customers may be uneasy about being asked to provide referrals. Your customers know they like your store, but they are not sure if they want to risk a relationship if someone has a bad experience. You can address and hopefully overcome these fears by sharing information about your store situation with them through either a letter or email that includes the following information:

- How much you value their business, and how you feel they can be an advocate, a Champion, for your store.
- Why you need referrals: how the continued quality of the store depends on their referrals. Tell them how much the success of your store has

come from referrals. You estimate that over 40 percent of your business comes from referrals. This reinforces the importance of referrals and makes people feel more comfortable about doing referrals.

- Guidance to your customers on whom they should talk to. Sometimes just referring to friends and family may not be as helpful as being more specific. Ask them to talk to "friends who are looking for a mechanic, friends who are not happy with their current salon, neighbors who might not know the types of ice cream we sell." You can also give your customers hints. Ask them to speak to someone that they know who loves fashion, someone interested in saving money; or someone who really likes great food. You are helping them put a picture of their friends who fit that profile in their minds, or you are giving them a key word to remember when a friend brings up a topic in conversation.
- What you will be doing with their referrals. Some of your customers might have had bad experiences with referrals in the past (such as aggressive and annoying sales calls). Ease any concerns and promise not to hound referrals. Tell them exactly the types of communications you will have with their friends and Family.

Never forget: Always acknowledge your customers' support. "We appreciate your business and we appreciate your support in letting others know about our store." *We cannot say this enough*: Be sure to thank your customer for every referral in order to keep the referral top of mind with your best customers.

At the same time, decide how Store Champions can help you track their referrals. One idea to consider is to provide Store Champions with a special card to give to the friends and family that they refer to the store. The card should have a space where the Store Champion can write in his or her name; the friend that they refer can then turn in the card to get a one-time discount or a special gift. By keeping track of cards redeemed, you will have a simple tally of who your active Store Champions are and how many referrals each of them has generated. You should also investigate whether you can set up some type of tracking for emails that your customers forward, perhaps tracking via a coupon or some other type of offer that new customers have to bring into the store. Also consider creating a "referred by" bulletin board in your store to recognize your champions.

Determine what type of rewards you will give to your Store Champions for their referrals. There are many ways you can thank Store Champions. One key reward is simply acknowledgment of the referral. A chiropractor has a sign in the office thanking all the patrons who have referred someone. This acknowledges them, plus it keeps the idea of making referrals top of mind whenever someone is coming into the store. Whatever you do, this reward should be highly personalized to recognize the unique relationship you have with these customers. Regardless of what type of reward you choose, you should always, *always* write a personal thank-you note to each person who refers a new customer to you. That is just good business. Additionally, think about thanking your Store Champions in a special section of your newsletter.

Here are some ideas for rewards that might be appropriate for your store champions:

If you are a . . .	Think about
Jewelry store	A referral lottery where all Store Champions are entered into a lottery (one entry per referral). Winner gets a high-value prize.
Hair salon, chiropractor, or pizza delivery restaurant	Same type of referral lottery, only winner gets a year's worth of services.
Sporting goods store	Invite all your Store Champions to tailgate party at a sporting event.
Deli, restaurant, wine shop, bookstore	Have a wine and cheese party for your Store Champions.

You can also send them a thank you in the form of a two-prong discount: one to keep for themselves and one to pass on to a friend. This keeps the referral process going.

Even though we anticipate that most of your referrals will come from your best customers, there are other ways that you can create a referral network within your community. Here are some ideas to think about and try to tweak for your own store:

- See if there is a way to create an event built on referrals. Our impetus for this idea is Ripe, a high-end restaurant. The only way to get a reservation at this great restaurant is to be invited by someone who has already dined at Ripe. You can use this same idea by allowing your key customers to invite a few friends to a fashion show, a wine tasting, a new product demonstration, or some other type of event. Your customers will need to print out and bring their invitation to be admitted to the event. You will be tracking the referral names as well as those key customers who instigated the referrals.
- Become an information source. Become known as an authority on your area and welcome all types of questions from all types of people: from the press, from interest groups, from noncustomers. Make connections with newspaper, radio, and television press and let them know you will be happy to answer any questions that they have about your area of expertise. Do not become the know-it-all expert on everything; instead, think about a specific area of expertise for which you can be known. Here are some examples.

If you are a . . .	Become the expert in:
Florist	Flowers for weddings
Auto mechanic	Certain types of cars (foreign, classic, etc.)
Pet store	Dog training; exotic pets
Dry cleaning	"Green" methods of dry cleaning
Hardware store	Basic home repairs

Another way to give a meaningful reward is to collaborate with a complimentary business and offer your Store Champions rewards that complement your own offerings. Some ideas on partner businesses are shown in Table 4-7.

Some retailers may think: "I gave those loyal customers a big discount. What else do they want?" Well, research today tells us that your customers are probably more sensitive to frequency than magnitude. To put it another way: How *often* you reward your customers is usually more important than how *much* you reward them.

This is important to consider because providing smaller rewards more frequently may be a better way for you to conduct business. However, you must also be aware of what your competitor is offering, and choose to either match or exceed their reward or offer a reward in a completely different class. Remember that creating loyalty is much broader than just offers or savings. Rewards are information, insight into your business, secrets or specials, and ways that you go about business. Some people, especially Champions, use this information to reinforce their choice and go out and talk up your store.

Which is the best program? It depends on a mix of several things: the types of consumers you are trying to reach and the attractiveness of the offer you are making. Keep in mind that the one that is best for you will be the one that is a balance of your interests and the consumers' interests. Frequent flyer programs

Table 4-7 Ideas for Partnering with Other Stores

If you are a	Partner with a	And give these types of rewards
Hair salon	Nail or tanning salon	Free service
Deli	Wine shop or kitchen store	Kitchen gadget or bottle of wine
Shoe store	Clothing store	One-time discount
Sporting goods store	Dry cleaners	Coupon for a free cleaning on camping equipment
Florist	Wedding gown store	Free wedding guest book
Auto repair shop	Car wash	Free car wash

Table 4-8 Rewards Approaches by Segment

The Segment	The Goal	Try This
Family	Maintain loyalty and encourage WOM	No matter what, you want to maintain good relationships and provide exceptional customer service. Develop a loyalty program that addresses their unique needs.
	Generate referrals	Start a referral program using the most loyal members of the Family.
Flirts	Increase loyalty	You want a program that will increase their frequency. Consider an interval or token economy program to increase the frequency and consistency of their visits.
	Begin WOM	Collect information to allow you to begin conversations with them (see Chapter 3). Suggest that they tell friends about the things you're telling them.
Phantoms	Induce visits	A continuous reinforcement program might get them to try your store, and offering a ratio or token economy program might encourage them to come back more than once.

Action Idea: Take out your marketing calendar/grid and look at the activities that you already have scheduled. Now look at one of the segments above and plan some activities in the next few months that focus specifically on that segment. Be sure to track the results. Reassess what you have done at the end of the period, and then devise a plan to continue for the next few months, and consider adding another target and goal at that time.

work for just this reason. From a consumer standpoint, the rewards are generous, albeit limited. The airline can justify these rewards because average award costs are closer to the direct costs of carrying a passenger (an extra meal, extra aircraft fuel, etc.) than to the actual cost of purchasing a comparable ticket. It works because there is a low likelihood that an award passenger will displace a paying passenger.

Think back to our three audience segments: the Family, the Flirts, and the Phantoms. What should you think about for each of them?

SUMMING UP

In this chapter, we have shown you:

- How to ask customers to tell others about your store.
- How to thank customers for talking about your store through reward programs.
- The difference between referral and reward programs.
- How to figure out which type of program is best for you.
- Many ideas on how to implement a program that is specific to your business.

It all goes back to understanding your customers. You might have noticed that there is one theme common to reward, loyalty, and referral programs: *connection*. You should use the program to connect with customers, and the way to do this is to know and understand your customers. A recent survey by Maritz Loyalty Marketing found that many retailers do not consistently connect with customers after they join a program,[10] and those retailers are missing a terrific opportunity to continue the customer dialogue and to encourage word-of-mouth efforts.

We have spent the first part of this book talking about customers and conversations. Now it is time to talk about strengthening those bonds and turning your customers into a community.

Chapter **5**

How Customer Communities Work

Customers → Conversations → *Community* → Commitment

You have engaged your best customers with your store, your brand. You have used word of mouth to get your best customers to talk to others in their social networks (their friends, their families, and their colleagues) about your store. What is the next step? It is for your store and your brand to be a catalyst that enables people to engage in conversations with people they do not yet know in new, sometimes surprising, but always meaningful ways. What will happen? You will create a community of customers. We consider this to be the new wave in word-of-mouth marketing.

The next few chapters are all about communities: what they are, what they can do for you and for your customers, and how you can develop a community. In this chapter, the Getting Started section will go over some basic definitions, while the Moving Forward section will provide you with a few mini–case studies on how other marketers have created communities. In the Taking It Further section, we will talk about how communities can affect your bottom line. The subsequent chapters contain more detailed information on setting up your community.

One of the most surprising things that we have found while writing this book is that very few retailers, regardless of whether they are big or small, have embraced the idea of community. In early 2007, it is difficult to find good examples of communities developed and supported by retailers. We think that fact should be considered a fabulous opportunity for you. You are not going to have a lot of competition from other retail communities, and you will be catching the early wave of what is an important element of society today. So join us in learning all about communities.

GETTING STARTED: CUSTOMER COMMUNITIES AS THE THIRD PLACE

There are many definitions of *community*. A basic one states that a community is a group of people who share social interaction and some common ties and who share an area (that is, a physical space) for some of the time. Sociologist Ray Oldenburg developed this definition with his idea of community as a "great good place," which he also describes as the "third place" that exists and is used in our everyday lives. The third place is the place other than one's home and one's workplace. In this third place, we put our differences (such as race and class) aside to meet with members of our community. Think of the TV show *Cheers*—you are thinking about a community; a place that welcomes many different kinds of people and, well, where everybody knows your name. A third place is not just a bar or tavern, though; a third place could be any place that is relatively inexpensive or free to get in to. It could be a community center, a church, a restaurant, or a retail store. On the other hand, it could be an online meeting place. What are most important are the ties that the third places provide for us.

Communities do not necessarily need a physical space to develop. Sometimes communities form based on the interests of a particular group of people. We live in a world of affinity communities: book clubs, knitting circles, running groups, British car enthusiasts. An informal group of people decide to get together and meet, and during the course of the group meeting, the members will not only talk about books or knitting or running or British cars, but also restaurants and movies and all the little brand discussions that are pervasive in our social interactions. The group also looks for a permanent place to meet, either in real space or Internet space, because interacting with the community is important.

Your store is a customer community. You provide the space and opportunity for members of the community to meet and talk. You and your employees are a part of the community, as are your customers. So you are connecting customers who may or may not know each other but are likely to have things in common to talk about—not just your store but also the other interests in their lives.

Communities tend to thrive because they allow for the telling of stories. The idea of storytelling is an old one, but it has recently been adopted by numerous large corporations as a way to develop a customer-centric company culture. Customer stories show us ways to talk to customers both for the short term and in the long term. Stories also work to strengthen your word-of-mouth campaigns in that your customers can use other customers' stories in their discussions and talks with their friends, family, and colleagues. Stories thus provide a continual freshness of ideas. You can use your customer stories to see customers' wants and needs and to evaluate current and future success for your store.

Brand stories are in the spotlight today because of the rise of consumer generated content on the Internet. What are blogs, viral videos, and a page on MySpace if they are not an individual's stories about their lives, often including all the information and stories about all the brands with which they interact?

However, brand stories and a consumer community are not just for the Internet. In the next few chapters, we will show you online and offline strategies for creating community.

GETTING STARTED: UNDERSTANDING THE CUSTOMER BENEFITS OF COMMUNITIES

We talked in the first chapter about all the reasons you should consider getting involved with a customer community. We want to talk now about what is in it for customers.

- **Connections.** The simple fact is that communities allow people to talk with each other. Today, Americans have fewer close confidants than in the past due to the facts that they are working longer and commuting for longer times to get to the workplace.[1] That is why certain types of communities, specifically online communities, are becoming more popular: They allow for a very real need for humans to connect.
- **Empowerment.** Communities empower customers by giving them the ability to be heard and the knowledge that you hear what they say. Customers learn that others share their hopes, fears, dreams, likes, and dislikes. They become more confident in discussing issues with others. When you participate in the discussion, you are doing several things. You are helping address some of their concerns and being part of the dialogue. By doing this, customers know that they are being heard in a way that can have an impact on their lives.
- **Trust.** Communities build trust. *Trust* is a reliance on something (such as information) or someone based on past experiences. Communities allow others' past experiences to help customers learn and make decisions about things that are of interest to them. Trust is often based on the quantity and quality of information gathered during an interaction with others in the community. The more trust one feels in the community, the greater the possibility that one will share information with others, and the greater the possibility that others will act on their advice. Trust can also be described as the "willingness of one party to be vulnerable to the actions of another."[2] This definition has two underlying dimensions: credibility and benevolence. *Credibility* is an individual's belief in the expertise of the person giving the information. *Benevolence* is perceptions regarding that person's concern about the consumer's best interest.[3] Clearly, the dialogue generated by a community goes a long way toward establishing a high level of trust among members of the community.
- **Advice.** The discussions and ideas that come out of a community are more than the sum of a group of individual opinions. Communities thrive on interactions: People in communities build upon ideas, provide deep insights

into their own wants and needs, and provide important information that help them improve their shopping experiences. Thus, people in a community receive much more information and advice than those not in the community. Along with this advisor role comes an increase in collective control of the community. Most brand communities have a strictly informal structure in terms of their hierarchy, that is, if they have any type of hierarchy at all. It is important for you to recognize this unique nature of community, because you will have to give up a bit of control over information flow. Additionally, when you begin a community, you are making an implicit agreement with community members that their input will be valuable to you.

MOVING FORWARD: BEST PRACTICES OF CUSTOMER COMMUNITIES

We will warn you up front: Setting up a community is not a short-term project. Although you can establish a community fairly quickly, you must commit to nurturing and supporting the community during its lifetime. The good news is that you can use a lot of the things you have been doing for your word-of-mouth marketing to build and nurture your community.

Regardless of whether you decide to develop a community that is online or offline, there are a few basic best practices that you should think about before implementing any type of community.

Best Practice 1: Understand the Importance of Social Glue

What is social glue? It is the basic thing that enables communities to function as communities. It is the shared interests that are relevant to members of the community. Soccer is the social glue for Latin and South Americans. Shared beliefs are the social glue for some religious communities. High school is the social glue for teenagers. Scott Bedbury refers to these key commonalities as "brand touchstones."[4]

Starbucks was one of the first companies to embrace Oldenburg's idea of a great good place. Starbucks CEO Howard Schultz refers to Starbucks as the third place of American life: a place without stresses of home or office, a neutral place where you will always finds friends (either on the sofa or behind the counter).[5] Starbucks analyzed the long tradition of coffee houses in the United States and Europe after they realized that for most people, the idea of coffee was more than a product to be consumed. Starbucks decided then to create a community that elevated the experience around drinking a cup of coffee. Its social glue, then, was not the coffee itself, but the experience of drinking it. Bedbury describes Starbucks' brand touchstone as "rewarding everyday moments."[6] This touchstone helps us understand what being part of the Starbucks community means: the coffee experience is a reward that happens as part of one's daily life.

The Starbucks experience—the comfortable chairs, the good lighting, the music and the newspapers—all promote this positive experience. Starbucks welcomes groups who gather to discuss books and music; they also offer books and music for purchase in their stores. Online, you can join discussion groups at the Starbucks Web site.

This interesting idea of a third place has been used by a number of different types of retailers: bookstores and craft stores now provide food, beverages, and a place to sit and interact. Union National Bank took the Starbucks concept to heart and to the lobby of a new location in Harrisburg, Pennsylvania. This new branch features a coffee shop integrated into the bank, where frontline bank employees are both bankers and baristas. Like Starbucks, the bank offers a place for customers to sit down and spend time; they offer publications, WiFi access, and large-screen TVs with a variety of programming, including information on the bank's offerings. It is open seven days a week. The bank/café, located near a college campus, is looking to forge deep relationships with the community where it is located by providing a community space. In doing so, it created a differentiation between both the coffee and the banking experience.[7]

How does social glue translate to the Internet environment? What do you do when you do not have a physical space where people can gather? Simply this: You find a social glue that people will relate to. We recommend that you do not base the community on the sole idea that you have a store. Building a community around the fact that people shop at your store probably will not resonate with your customers. Instead, look for the relevant commonalities between both your business and your customers. Is it food, sports, kids? Is it being up to the minute on fashion, books, movies? Is it decorating, cooking, and traveling? Spend a few minutes brainstorming and you will probably find some key commonalities on which to build your community. Here is an example. It is a community developed by Kraft Foods, the company that makes macaroni and cheese and Miracle Whip.

Everyone has to eat, so it is only natural that many communities are built around food. At Kraft Foods' Web site, for example, you will find an online message board and a recipe exchange. Both areas include content generated from members of the Kraft Foods staff and from community members themselves. The Kraft Foods site includes discussions on cooking, ingredients, shortcuts, and how to get fussy kids to eat. The value is that you can see what topics customers are most interested in, and you can use this information to think about new offerings for them. The Kraft recipe database contains more than 15,000 recipes, and recipes are not required to contain Kraft products. The recipes are also rated by other members of the forum so that information can be used to make decisions. This type of ratings system helps customers make decisions, and it also enhances feelings of community because the online members are on an equal footing with one another—anyone can rate a recipe whether they are a top chef, a Kraft nutritionist, or a new mom.

The Kraft online message board sites are moderated but not censored. This means that there is someone who monitors the conversations. Most private communities are facilitated by a moderator (or by several moderators), who is seen as the voice of the company that sponsors the community. The value of good moderators is that they keep the discussion lively, introduce new topics that engage the members in meaningful conversations, moderate activities that provide insights for the sponsoring company, and help new members (known as newbies) fit in to the community. Good moderators also observe patterns among the community and are able to postulate what these might mean to the company's business strategy.

Are you saying to yourself: "Hey, my store is nothing like Kraft Foods! I can't do something like that!" But you can! One example of a retailer starting a community is the Bass Pro Shops, a small chain of sporting good stores focusing on hunting, fishing, and other outdoor pursuits. They sponsor a large online community devoted to these activities; check it out at forums.basspro.com/cgi-bin/ultimatebb.cgi. You will find, for example, a forum dedicated to fly fishing. In this forum, customers post places they like to fish, the types of reels they like and dislike, and directions for tying flies. You will notice that some of the topics are related to the products they sell, some are not. But the customers are reminded of the forum sponsors whenever they visit, and that can create a valuable impression among customers.

So how do begin to develop your community? What is the "social glue" that you build your community around? To get started, ask yourself these questions.

- What is unique about my business? Is it my product mix? Do I sell something that no one else does in my area? Are people interested enough in this to spend time talking about it with others? Do I sell collectibles that people will want to talk about? Do I use ingredients that are unique and special that people will be interested in? If so, think about a community based around interest in collectibles or in your special ingredients. Do I sell something that is particularly natural or healthy? Certain people are looking for the newest health information out there. Do I sell many locally made products? If so, think about building a community based around the history of your local community and support for local manufacturers, producers or artisans. Does my restaurant sell the freshest fish, make the most innovative desserts, have the most complete wine list? If so, think about creating a special gourmet group that meets regularly to try new offerings.
- Do I have access to special information sources? Do I sell things related to someone's hobby or job or family? Do I have sources of information that can benefit people that shop at your store? Do I have customers who are experts and are willing to share their expertise? If so, consider a community built around providing this unique information.
- What are my employees and I interested in? What do my employees like to do in their free time? Is this something that I'm interested in? If you share a passion with your employees, you might be able to share that passion with your customers via a unique community.

What you have probably noticed as you have thought about these things is that your community will not be all things to all people. That is not a problem at all. If you are having problems figuring out your social glue, keep going back to your customer research and see how you can match your community to the interests of the best customers of your store. Then you can rely on them to engage others with their interests. We will get to that in a moment.

Best Practice 2: Invite People to Join Your Community

Once you have decided the role of your community and the social glue that your community will offer, you need to invite the right people to join it. Invite those customers with a common interest in your community, who have a passion for the social glue, and who are willing to participate. People join communities to share and celebrate their similarities and to be something bigger than themselves. How many people should be in your community? There is no set number; the more important thing is that they all have an interest in the community and in keeping it going.

In an online situation, you will want to have people register to join and participate in the community. This serves several purposes. People who believe that their community is not open to all and somewhat private will be more apt to participate in conversations, and they will feel more comfortable in an environment where they know what they see will be seen by others in the community. You can use your community to learn about the other key interests that community members might have or want, using polls or survey techniques as described in the Toolbox section. Additionally, registration will allow you to track the activities and conversations of the members and to make decisions about your store based on what they are talking about. If your community is built in-store, you can start by inviting people to events that will be held in your store and encourage the community to develop that way. In both an in-store and an online community, there will be drop-ins who just happen to be in the store. If they have an interest in what is going on, then encourage them to stay and be part of the community.

One of the oldest brand communities in existence is the Harley-Davidson Owners Group (HOG). When people purchase a Harley-Davidson, they are invited to join the national organization, which consists of hundreds of small, local groups of riders. These groups are usually organized by the local retailer, and group activities are geared around the interests of the owners, in addition to riding their Harleys. Some HOG groups have done fundraising (such as organizing a rally to raise funds for the Asian tsunami victims), organized political protests (such as group rallies against helmet laws), and community service activities. Thus, the social glue provides the guidelines of whom to invite to be in the group, and the social glue leads to a second layer of social glue, based on the individual characteristics of the members.

How do you create a community when your customers are all over the world? If you are Starwood Hotels, you create an Internet presence for your newest hotel brand. The brand, Aloft, targets design-conscious and tech-savvy travelers. These hotels will feature a unique range of offerings including wireless Internet access, a lounge with electronic entertainment kiosks, in-room plug and play connectivity units, and free document printing. Rooms are all loft-style, and guests can select their rooms from a number of floor plans, all searchable interactively online when a reservation is made. To generate excitement about Aloft, Starwood invited customers to visit an online prototype of the hotel at the popular Second Life virtual world. Guests could watch the virtual hotel being built, and joined in conversations to talk about the types of things that would interest them in staying at the hotel. So far, more than 500,000 of these guests, all previous visitors to a Starwood hotel, have registered at the new cyber-hotel. Starwood's hope is that this will transfer into real-life visits when the first Alofts open in 2008.[8]

Another example is a small accessories retailer called 1154 Lill Studio, which has shops in Boston, Chicago, and Kansas City, as well as an online presence (www.1154lill.com). This company has enhanced its relationships with current and prospective customers by hosting events where people can create their own purses: they pick the style, the fabric, and the embellishments, and then the purses are custom made by the store's factory in Chicago and shipped to the partygoers in about three weeks. Some of these events are at their stores after hours, and some are at customers' homes. The party hostess gets a discount on her bag, and all party guests feel that they are a part of both the company and the community.

Action Idea: In the next chapters, we will provide you with instructions that are more specific for setting up your community. For now, think about your existing points of customer contact and plan to announce and invite people to your community. Ways to do this include:

- A special email with information about the goals and purposes of the community. Of course, include a link to the site of the community.
- An article in your newsletter that talks about the goals of your community.
- Information in your print advertisements about the community.

Best Practice 3: Encourage Openness

As we have mentioned before, part of the value of community is that people in the community will build upon the information and conversations that you facilitate. Therefore, it is important that you, as a key communicator in the community, be genuine in your conversations and encourage openness and honesty. You will want to reinforce their participation in the community with positive feedback, which will empower people to discuss things even more. A simple "great idea" or "terrific story" comment will have people knowing that you listen to them. You can also use key employees as additional moderators to reduce the amount of responding you will have to do personally.

We have talked a lot in this book about rewarding customers, and you probably have some good thoughts on how you can reward your loyal customers. To create more of a community feel, think about some intangible rewards for the participants in your community. There's a small company that makes energy bars called Luna Bars, which are 100 percent natural and formulated to provide optimal nutrition for women. Luna Bars encourage their customers to write personal dedications to other women who have touched their lives in some way. These dedications, mailed in to Luna or posted on their Web site, are then reviewed, and some of the best dedications are selected to be printed on the back of a Luna Bar wrapper. Luna has also woven some of the dedications into a quilt that they take with them to sponsored events. Luna executives feel that creating these dedications and seeing them on the Luna Web site makes customers feel like they are part of the Luna family. It keeps customers passionate, and it also keeps the people who work at Luna passionate.

Action Idea: Think about ways to recognize members of your community once they join, such as:

- A personalized thank-you email when they register.
- A small button or sticker given as a gift to new members.
- An electronic button that members can put on their blogs to show that they belong.

Best Practice 4: Create Community-Building Activities

Communities can need a bit of help to get going. One way is to create community-building activities that help people understand what the community is about. These activities can accomplish several goals: They encourage participation in the community that is more structured, which can make people feel more comfortable participating in less structured conversations, and they allow people to get to know each other over time. The activities also reinforce the social glue of your community. In the previous example of Luna Bar, we showed you how an activity at a Web site can also serve as a reward or recognition of community membership. The next chapters give you many ideas on the types of community activities you could create.

The electronics store Best Buy created a store within a store at a suburban Chicago location. The store within a store, called Studio D, is designed to attract women shoppers, not the core base of Best Buy's business. Studio D features a limited assortment of merchandise built around digital cameras, one of the few electronics categories that women have enthusiastically embraced. Studio D hires no-pressure, consultative salespeople who work in a way modeled after Nordstrom's. Studio D creates community by recognizing women as the family record keepers, and thus offers classroom workshops and in-store special events to recognize this role. For example, recent workshops included "Discovering Your iPod" and "Creating Family Calendars." The activities give customers new skills and Best Buy executives have noticed that they create a sense of community that encourages repeat visits.[9] Other Studio D stores in more urban areas (with fewer soccer mom customers) will focus on health and well-being.

Action Idea: Think about the types of information that will be of most interest to people in your community. Then you can think of a hands-on activity based on that information, such as an interactive quiz, that allows community members to interact with the information.

Best Practice 5: View People in Your Community as Advisors

As you create your community, you need to view the people in your community more like advisors to your company rather than a market research panel. You have already instigated the one-on-one conversations that get you important research data. Now, let the good ideas of your customers grow through their interactions with each other. This does not mean that you are not part of the conversation, in fact, your presence is very important to keep the conversations flowing. Respond to ideas, ask questions about the things that people are talking about, and let them know what you are doing with the information that they are talking about. The more you respond, the more people will help your company. Think of it as a perpetual improvement loop,[10] where every comment is built on and elaborated on to help you learn more.

Shouldice Hospital in Thornhill, Ontario, is a small hospital that focuses on hernias. For the past sixty years, the hospital has hosted an annual gala where former hernia patients are invited to dinner, entertainment, and a quick physical examination of their surgery site. The gala is organized by a committee of former patients. The hospital performs more than thirty hernia operations a day and has a 99 percent success rate with these surgeries. It focuses on building community by encouraging patients to meet one another and share experiences that make the hospital stay much less frightening than it can be. The feedback from the people in the community is used to improve every facet of the hospital. The success of the community-building aspect is seen in that half of the new patients at the hospital were referrals from former patients.[11]

Action Idea: Think about the feedback mechanisms that you have in place, and consider how you will use those to recognize people in your community. Keep track of the feedback so you can see how customer responses change (hopefully for the better) as the community develops.

Best Practice 6: Use a Mix of Technology and Methodology, and Keep Trying New Things

For many of the examples we have given you, you will note that a mix of efforts was employed. Kraft uses online methods, but uses both a message board and a recipe exchange. Luna uses dedications on its Web site, on wrappers, and on the traveling quilt. A mix of technologies and methodologies allows multiple entry points for people to join your community, and once people find the right place to interact, it is likely that they will venture into other places to be part of the community.[12] It also allows a richer experience for both you and your customers. Remember when we talked about communities as a way for people to tell their stories? Not everybody will want to tell their story in the same way. So offering multiple ways for people to tell stories will help establish and nurture your community.

In 2006, Hallmark Cards wanted to find a way to get people to talk and connect with each other, and also noted the rise of social networking sites like YouTube, which allows people to share videos they create in an online environment. Hallmark decided that it wanted input from customers to develop content for both its Web site and television channel (the Hallmark Channel). They started an effort called "Tell Us Your Story," which invites viewers of the Hallmark Channel (and visitors to their Web site) to submit stories of a romantic moment or an expression of love, or other topical theme. The stories can be either video stories à la YouTube or traditional written stories. The company will select ten and produce short animated videos to air on the network and the Web site starting in February 2007. February, as you know, has the Valentine's Day holiday, and Hallmark plans a full month of romantic movies during that time. Such an effort will allow viewers to become part of the Hallmark family, with the benefits of driving traffic to the Hallmark Web site, and will help Hallmark provide significant amounts of content to help viewers connect and understand each other.[13]

> **Action Idea:** Look at your annual marketing plan/grid and think about the times of the year when the community is most likely to want to get involved with your social glue. Plan your community activities during slow periods, or during times when you do not have many sales promotion activities happening. Look at the traditional advertising vehicles you have in place and consider ways to use these vehicles to promote and nurture your community.

Best Practice 7: Embrace All Feedback, Both Positive and Negative

When you have a community that is open and honest, where all input is valued, and where people are encouraged to speak their minds, it is likely that you will hear bad things about your store. Your first reaction when conversation turns negative will naturally be to stop it: to change the subject if you are with your community members in person, to cut off an online chat if your community is online. But squelch that impulse! Negative feedback is at least as important, and probably more important, than the positive feedback you hear.

While negative feedback is certainly a valid concern, it is also a realistic situation in the retailing world today. Chances are someone, somewhere is going to say something negative about you, and it is probably better that they say something negative in your own community than in a situation where you have no control over what is happening.

Negative communication in your community can be a terrific learning experience for you. You should use that information to listen, learn, respond, and revise. If one customer has a problem or an issue, chances are that others (either within or without) of the community are also experiencing it.[14] By listening to the negative feedback, learning more about it, and responding to it, you will strengthen the ties you have with your community members and increase the level of trust that your community has in you and your store. You also give them more good information to talk about to others in their personal networks.

The computer retailer CompUSA recently decided to add customer reviews to its Web site. While user reviews are popular on shopping search engines like CNET, only a few retailers (like Amazon.com) have utilized customer reviews, as retailers naturally see bad reviews as deterrents to product sales. However, CompUSA believed the presence of negative product assessments would improve customer loyalty over the long term. To encourage customers to give reviews, CompUSA instigated a promotion where everyone writing a review was entered in a drawing to win cash. The reviews had a positive impact both on conversions and average order value. Visitors who read the company's product reviews were 50 percent more likely to convert than those who did not. And those same people spent an average 20 percent more per order than the typical customer.

Negative reviews of products and of the store itself is seen as a way to improve quality control and customer service at CompUSA. When the information offered on a product description page did not match the actual product, customers posted the discrepancy in reviews, after which CompUSA spoke with the manufacturer and corrected the error. And then they told everyone on their community site about it, further developing their store credibility and engendering trust among their customers.

Action Idea: You have probably already spent time responding to comments, and it is important to continue, be the comments positive or negative. Practice responding to negative criticisms so you do not have an automatic, emotional reaction. When your visitors see that you listen to what they are saying, they will appreciate your efforts. They will begin to provide feedback and commentary that is more thoughtful, and they will look forward to your responses.

TAKING IT FURTHER: UNDERSTANDING HOW COMMUNITIES PAY OFF FOR YOUR STORE

How do you know whether to make the commitment to a customer community? We have given you our thoughts on how communities can benefit both your store and your customers. But we are sure you are wondering: Do communities affect your business' bottom line? Creating and maintaining a community will take some time and money. Is it really going to be worth it?

We have already talked about how communication increases customer loyalty. In a similar way communities will make your customers more knowledgeable about your store and should increase their loyalty to your store. It will also give them more things to talk about with people in their personal social networks. While it is hard to indicate the actual impact to the bottom line, a recent study regarding eBay can help quantify the effects of community on the bottom line.

A recent experiment at the German eBay site was designed to see if communities really paid off for customers. Researchers identified about 140,000 eBay members who had been active in the auction portion of the site but did not belong to any online communities. They invited half of them to join a customer community. Within three months, about 15,000 of these eBay members were participating in the community, about 3,000 of them as active participants who posted messages, answered questions, and joined discussions. The remaining members were lurkers, those people who read other people's posts but rarely participated.

The researchers examined the behavior of these 15,000 people during the course of a year. They found that both the active participants and the lurkers bid twice as often as those who were not part of the community. They spent more than 50 percent more money than those not part of the community. The active members listed four times as many items as those not in a community. Combined, the activities of active members and lurkers resulted in 56 percent more sales during the year than in the previous one.[15]

In addition, it is possible that creating a strong community can mitigate many of the problems associated with traditional marketing approaches and may cause you to rethink your spending in traditional advertising media. You will not have to be concerned with message clutter and media fragmentation, thus reducing your need for a campaign with a high frequency of exposure in traditional media. You might think about foregoing a direct marketing campaign with minimal return on investment.

SUMMING UP

In this chapter, we showed you:

- What a community is and how it functions as a third place for your customers.
- The benefits of community to your customers.

- Best practices for community building, including how to decide on your social glue, invite people to your community, encourage openness, create activities, use advisors, try new things, and deal with negative feedback.
- How communities can pay off.

At this point, we hope you see that you can create and support a community. While many of the examples we discussed in this chapter were communities begun by large corporations with great resources to spend on getting the community up and running, we think many of the lessons from these case studies can easily be applied to your own local store. We also think that communities can appeal to the Family, the Flirts, and the Phantoms, especially if you can connect to them on their personal interests, rather than specifically to something about your store brand. We will show you more about this in upcoming chapters.

Chapter **6**

Establishing Your Online Community

Customers → Conversations → *Community* → Commitment

In the previous chapter we gave you some information on why and how communities work. In this chapter, we provide some step-by-step instructions, along with lot of examples, to get you going on your community. Right off the bat, we recommend that you create an online community—a virtual community— for your store. It is not as hard or as demanding as you think. There are several ways to develop an online community: through discussion boards, blogs, and more. In the Getting Started section, we will describe each of these types of communities and give you some examples of each. If you are already familiar with these types of online offerings, just move ahead to the details on how to establish your online community in the Moving Forward section. Once you have a community established, take a look at the Taking It Further section for some advanced considerations about your community. Then, in the next chapter, we will talk about how to support your online community with different activities in your store and your community.

GETTING STARTED: SUCCESSES AND CHALLENGES OF ONLINE COMMUNITIES

Just what exactly is an online community? An online community is a group of people who use computer networks as their primary mode of interaction. It is important to remember at this point that the Internet is one of the many ways in which people interact; it is not a separate reality. People online have the same baggage as people offline. Like your in-store community, an online (or virtual) community will involve a sense of commonality, that is, a common purpose, interest, or set of objectives—you know, the social glue. In a virtual community, your community members are providing the content, and we will give you information later in this chapter on how to get that going.

In its simplest form, an online community is just another example of word of mouth. Many of your customers will be interested in the experience of other shoppers and will use that information to make decisions in addition to the information provided by you, producers, or advertisements.[1] In fact, consumers view text information found in online forums easier to use and more trustworthy than other types of information.

The Internet as a media channel is an expert facilitator of communities and builds relationships both online and in the real community where participants live. A study by Hampton (2001) found that Internet users know more local residents, talk with twice as many people, and are more likely to invite neighbors into their homes than people who do not use the Internet.[2] Another study showed that the Internet supplements a range of different communications: interpersonal communication with family and friends, organizational involvement, and political participation. These findings have been confirmed by several other studies.[3] Thus, the Internet not only provides a place to have a community, it also serves to strengthen existing ties in the real, physical community.

In addition to this, there are numerous reasons to establish an online community:

- *People love online communities.* Online communities are very popular and are growing in popularity. Initially, such networks were developed due to the need for information retrieval and sharing.[4] However, they have grown to include a large number of affinity groups that bring together people looking for that important social glue. There are communities dedicated to almost any type of group you can imagine: *Star Wars* fans, knitters, dog lovers, you name it. We discussed in Chapter 5 why people are interested in communities, and the Internet is a no-boundaries way for important connections to be made.

- *People who use communities tend to shop a lot.* Online community participants tend to shop at online stores. People who contribute product reviews or post messages visit community Web sites at online stores nine times more often than sites without communities, remain twice as loyal, and buy almost twice as often. Even customers who read but do not contribute to community interaction are more frequent visitors and buyers. It is likely that this sense of community can translate to your real store.[5]

- *People can participate in a community at any hour of any day.* The online community is open and possibly active twenty-four hours a day, seven days a week. The great value to this type of asynchronous communication is that people can participate in the community on their own time. Online communities are also not constrained by physical limitations. You may only be able to accommodate a dozen people around the table in your store, but you can welcome hundreds of people to an online community.

- *Communities are sources of credible information.* The lack of face-to-face contact in an online community may cause people to be more open and candid with their comments and feedback. Many social networks, though, focus on establishing social capital: a common set of expectations, shared values, and sense of trust among people in the network.[6] Participation in a social network, then, can strengthen a member's social contacts, and their feelings of engagement and attachment in a community.

However, there are some important challenges you need to be aware of in an online community.

- *People in your community are not currently in your store.* The community members are not physically in your store unless, of course, you provide a number of computer terminals for people to work on. As part of your role in the community, then, you will need to find ways to remind people to visit your store. We will give you some ideas on how to do that in Chapter 7.
- *The people in your community may not even be in your town.* The global nature of the Internet means that not everyone who participates in your community will be local. Thus, members of your community may not be able to shop at your store.
- *You will have to give up a bit of control in your community.* Because the community is likely to be bigger than your in-store customer base, and because you will not be online all the time, you will have much less control over the discussions that are going on. This just means you will have to be comfortable with less control than in an in-store community.
- *You may need a specialist to help with your community.* You will need to be comfortable with technology or be able to rely on someone who is comfortable with technology to set up and monitor your community.
- *People might not participate in your community.* The success of a community lies in the participation of its members. However, it can be a temptation for people to take resources from the group and to not give back. In Internet terms, this can be seen as the possibility that an individual will join the group as a lurker and not as an active participant. We will discuss how to deal with lurkers later on in this chapter.

We think the issues and most of the pitfalls of online communities can be overcome, particularly in light of the benefits that an online community can bring you.

MOVING FORWARD: CHOOSING A FORMAT FOR YOUR ONLINE COMMUNITY

There are a number of steps that you need to take in order to get your community up and running. The first is to choose a format in order to create a space for your community.

There are numerous ways that you can provide a format and create an online space for your community. We have listed resources for many of these at the end of this chapter and have many more at our Web site, www.underdog network.com. Three popular types are online message boards, blogs, and social networking sites.

Message Boards

Message boards are also known as online discussion groups, bulletin boards, and forums. In these types of communities, members can post and respond to all messages on the forum. Below are some examples of how retailers have used message boards.

- Bass Pro Shop Forums allow people to talk about hunting, fishing, and all kinds of other outdoor activities: forums.basspro.com/cgi-bin/ultimatebb.cgi.
- The Starbucks Book Club welcomes anyone who reads a book selected by Starbucks and wants to discuss it: starbucks.gather.com.
- The Hot Topic community boards are populated by Hot Topic customers, who are teens and young adults interested in fashion and music: community.hottopic.com/beheard.asp?LS=0&.

Blogs

Blogs, or Web logs, are Web sites where individuals make entries in a journal or diary format and displayed in reverse chronological order. Some blogs provide commentary or news on a particular subject, such as food, politics, or local news. Other blogs act as more personal online diaries. A blog can combine text, images, and links to other blogs, Web pages, and other media related to its topic. Most blogs are primarily textual.

By 2006, about 34 percent of all corporate Web sites provided some type of blog. More than 5 percent of the *Fortune* 500 companies have some type of corporate blog. The growth continues, and it is likely that by the time you are reading this book that more than half of all large companies will have a corporate blog. Here are some examples:

- The blog at Armani Exchange is where fashion, music, and culture meet, and provides a daily dose of celebrity gossip: www.styletraxx.com.
- Kpixie, a yarn store, hosts a blog where new products are previewed and reviewed: www.pixieknit.com/blog.
- The Whole Foods Market blog is written by the grocery store's CEO and contains information on Whole Foods business policies. Each post gets

dozens of comments from interested readers: www.wholefoodsmarket.com/blogs/jm.

Social Networking Sites

A recent marketing phenomenon is the growth of social networking sites like MySpace and Facebook. Started as ways for young people to meet new friends and develop social connections online, marketers have recently begun to create pages on MySpace in order to be in the same electronic community where customers and potential customers spend time. These sites allow marketers to provide fun information in a multimedia environment. The cultural currency of social networking sites is friends Individuals will ask to be a friend of the site, and the number of friends that a site has is an indication of its popularity. Friends can leave comments, but there is minimal interaction.

- The Burger King MySpace page has images, games, videos, and many friends. At this writing, almost 136,000 people were signed up as friends of the Burger King: http://www.myspace.com/burgerking.
- The Bastille, a bar and restaurant in California, uses MySpace to promote upcoming specials and bands. It has almost 300 friends: www.myspace.com/100000002.
- Jewelry marketer Punster has a space with more than 8,000 friends: www.myspace.com/pugsterinc.

Regardless of the type of community you establish, you will have a level of trust among your customers who already know you and trust you. It is important not to downplay the store's role in setting up and maintaining the community because of this trust issue. Beyond that, the options all have pros and cons, as we have outlined in Table 6-1.

MOVING FORWARD: IDENTIFYING SOCIAL GLUE TO BRING YOUR COMMUNITY TOGETHER

Once you have decided on your community format and you are ready to get going with your virtual community, the next decision is to select your social glue. Put another way, you need to decide upon the content or topic that will be the focus of the interactions of your community. We have discussed the types of social glue that you can consider in the following chapters. Our review of different sites has found several types of glue that seem to have worked well for other companies in the virtual environment.

Table 6-1 Pros and Cons of Online Communities

	Message Boards	Blogs	Social Network
Level of interactivity	High: anyone can post and respond	Moderate: you control who can post, but anyone can respond to your posts	Moderate: anyone can respond to your postings
Focus on social glue	Moderate: discussions can wander off fairly easily	High: your control over postings ensures that social glue is front and center	Moderate
Amount of time/energy needed	High: without maintenance, may get out of control	Moderate: regular postings can take a few minutes per day	High: MySpace pages change their look frequently to give people a reason to keep coming back
Bells and whistles	Low	Moderate	High
Start-up cost	Moderate: most programs will charge for server capacity	None to moderate: several free and low-cost blogging programs are available	None to moderate: space is free, but some bells and whistles come with a cost
Users	Everyone online	Everyone online	Mostly younger people

Owner Groups

Set up an online community of individuals who own one of the products that you sell. For example, the Harley Owners Group (HOG) use the Web to pull together members of 1,200 local clubs in 100 countries around the world. The Web site provides information about clubs, and welcomes new members to the club. Harley provides information about all types of things, offers ideas, and relies on members as a direct source of feedback.

Obviously, certain things will be more likely to be social glue than others. For example, you probably will not get a lot of interest in a toothpaste owners group. However, other types of groups may generate more interest. Groups of people who own Mary Engelbreit products (or any other type of name-brand collectibles), people who love a double-double In-N-Out Burger, people who are big fans of your massage therapist and of massage in general might be willing to participate in a group dedicated to something they feel strongly about.

Here are some examples:

- A board for people who collect Hummel figurines www.worldcollectorsnet. com/hummel/hummelboard.html.
- A Subaru owner's club in the United Kingdom: www.scoobycity.co.uk/ phpBB2/portal.php.
- A board for Swatch watch owners www.worldcollectorsnet.com/swatch/ swatchboard.html.

Online Customer Interest/Support Groups

If you sell products in a specific category (health products, kids products, garden products), set up a community to address a range of questions around a general topic: an online parents group, a garden club, a support group for people with asthma or allergies. If you sell a product that is somewhat technical, think about setting up an online customer support group. Any type of electronics would be a natural for this, as well as mechanical products, cameras, crafts, and kitchen appliances. Topics can include how to fix or repair any minor problems or new ways to use the product. If you choose to do a blog, you can post about the information that you receive on new products and techniques. Here are some examples:

- An online community for crafters sponsored by Hancock Fabrics: p097. ezboard.com/bhancockfabrics.
- An online community for parents sponsored by *BabyCenter* magazine: www.babycenter.com.
- Information about car aftermarket products from the Web site automotive. com: forums.automotive.com.

Product Reviews

Another option is to invite customers to talk about all the different types of products you sell in your store. You can establish a rating system using stars or some other types of visual identifier to help people quickly see what others like and dislike. Some examples of communities that use this type of board are as follows.

- Reviews of books, CDs, movies, and more at Amazon.com: www. amazon.com.
- Reviews of crafting supplies at Hancock Fabrics: www.hancockfabrics. com/jump.jsp?itemID=757&itemType=CONTENT.

Ultimate Resource

Certain Web sites strive to be the ultimate resource for information on a certain topic. Do you want to be the best source of information for music, for decorating, for auto repair, for electronics? Like the Kraft Web site, registered community members can save recipes and other content in a personal folder, which keeps them coming back to the site.

- Anything you wanted to know, and more, about cake baking! An online community for cake bakers sponsored by a retailer called Cake Central: forum.cakecentral.com/cake-decorating-forums.html.
- All about produce and cooking at the Sainsbury's Grocery store forums: www.sainsburys.co.uk/yourideas/forums/30/ShowForum.aspx.

MOVING FORWARD: SELECTING THE BEST GLUE

If you are discovering one key area that your community will focus on, great! You are done and ready to move on to the next step. But what if you have several ideas and cannot decide? Home in on one or two things that might be of interest to most people.

Start by returning to your demographic and psychographic research that you conducted in the first phase of the development of your program (see Chapter 2).

What are some of the demographic and psychographic characteristics of your customers? Do you have many families with little kids? Many customers with two members of the household working full-time? Do you have more than an average number of Hispanics or another ethnic group? Is your store near a retirement home or do you have many older customers shopping at your store? Revisit some of the things that stood out on a demographic basis in those initial surveys. Seeing some strong trends in the direction of one demographic group or another can be enough to decide what types of support would work best for you.

Think also about the interests and lifestyles of your customers. See if you can spot any trends in your research regarding their hobbies or activities. Do they like outdoor activities? Which ones? Do they like to cook or decorate? Do they tend to have pets? Are they do-it-yourselfers? Do they like music or go to the movies often? Are they politically active? It is important to remember that you probably will not find a common interest for all of your customers, and that is fine. You want to find something that will engage a smaller group of people, and give them the opportunity to connect. You also want to have a community that will keep you and your staff interested, too. The number of people in your community is not as important as developing some level of engagement. This will lead to stronger word of mouth among the community members, as well as stronger bonds to your place of business.

Finally, think about things that you, yourself are interested in, and see if your interests match those of the people in your store. Say for a moment that you own a hardware store, and you love to cook. Does that mean you should *not* think about starting a gourmet community for your store? Not at all! It would be fascinating for people to talk about it: "Hey, I learned how to make this great appetizer at Joe's Hardware Store. He has all kinds of stuff for people who love to cook." Use your Store Champions to gauge their interest in such ideas and to judge whether such a community would be a success.

Using this information, narrow down to a few things that might be good for your social glue. To finalize your decision, think about these things:

- Is there a relationship between your store and the social glue? The connection should be there. If you own a sporting goods store, and you are interested in running, then you have a perfect fit. What if you own a sporting goods store and you are interested in baking? Not so perfect a fit. However, you could have a forum dedicated to healthy baking, and bring in other elements of a healthy lifestyle that are available at your store.
- Is there a match between your community glue and activities you can do in your store? For example, if you decide to establish a running forum, think about reaching out to runners (or skiers, or bikers) by creating a community based on that sport. Can you organize a running or biking group, or a regular set of ski outings? Can you organize a rally to support a charity or community cause? These types of outings can start and end at your store. The idea is to use the Internet to engage customers and bring them into your store. Table 6-2 shows some other ideas.

MOVING FORWARD: INVOLVING CUSTOMERS IN YOUR COMMUNITY

Communities need members. For an online community, you will need a critical mass to keep the community active and to hold the attentions of those

Table 6-2 Matching Community Glue and Activities at Your Store

If you have this type of store	If you have this kind of community	Get them in the store by
Hardware, DIY	Gardening	Arranging for garden tours that start and end at the store
Pet store	Pet care	Planning group dog walks or pet bathing demonstrations at the store
Hair salon, dry cleaners	Fashion-oriented	"Fashion crawl" where your group will visit hot fashion boutiques: meet at the salon for coffee before hand
Restaurant, deli, bakery	Food and wine	Vineyard tour: meet at store for indoctrination. Cooking class, recipe exchange, or a progressive dinner that starts and ends at the store

who are participating. Attrition will always occur, so you should be in a constant mode of inviting people to join the community.[7]

People choose to participate in communities for many different reasons. For some, participating in online communities is a natural act for them. These people are somewhat like online Flirts, active talkers in numerous different communities. Other things like an interest or passion in the topic, a desire for recognition from others, and a desire to give back to others are reasons why people join online communities.[8]

It is also important to recognize that while your in-store community consist of a tight circle of active participants, your online community will consist of people who are regular contributors and people who are lurkers—they read what other people say but never (or extremely rarely) participate in the discussion. In fact, on average about 15 percent of your community members will be active participants, and about 85 percent will be lurkers.

Action Idea: Take out your annual plan/marketing grid and look at your current communications channels and plans. Use those existing channels, both traditional advertising and the word-of-mouth activities that you have started, to invite people to join your community. Make it clear what the social glue is to your community, and let people know it is easy to use. You might even include some of the topics that are being discussed or that you plan to discuss at your community.

Make It Easy for Visitors to Get Involved

When people are first visiting your community, they are looking for some basic information to help them decide whether to join.[9] You should provide general information about the community in an easy-to-find Frequently Asked Questions file (also known as a FAQ). This is an important first step in developing trust in your online community. Specifically, they will want to know:

- Why they should join the community. Have you clearly articulated what your social glue will be?
- How do they join or leave? Have very clear instructions for registration, and include a statement about privacy and confidentiality.
- How do they read and send messages? Provide clear instructions on how to post, read, and respond to the community.
- Can they express themselves in ways other than with words? Are there options for people to post things other than text messages, such as images, links, and icons?
- Is the community safe? Is there some protection of personal information? We recommend that your community be private, that is, that people have to register to participate. Registration can consist simply of an email address as a login name and a password. There are several benefits to a private site. While public sites will have many more members, private sites

have a higher percentage of active participants.[10] Private communities create greater levels of trust and personal accountability among members, and they participate more often, add new ideas, and form connections. We will talk more about privacy protection in Chapter 10.

Encourage Members to Invite Others

Once you get a core group going at your community, take some steps with them to help you get the word out at your community.

- Ask them in a message on the forum or on the blog to invite friends to visit.
- Perhaps even give them a referral bonus or some type of recognition when someone that they have invited joins.
- Create a button that people can put on their blogs or on their personal Web sites to show they are part of the community. The button should direct people to your community. Here's a site where you can download free buttons: /www.crystalbuttons.com.
- Always discuss the online community in your newsletter and other types of messages that you send out.

You may wish to think about establishing some community rules or policies to post on your Web site. This will inform all members about the expectations of the community members regarding behaviors at the site. For example, will you ban anyone who makes a personal attack on other members? Do you need a disclaimer? Figallo recommends some basic fundamental rules for a community:

- Posters take responsibility for the words they post.
- Posting illegally obtained information is not permitted.
- Posting copyrighted information is not permitted (unless the poster owns the copyright).
- Posting pornography or other illegal information is prohibited.
- Harassment of others is not allowed.[11]

You can also check the Web sites of the different communities we have discussed in this section to see what kinds of rules they have posted for their own communities. You can adapt these rules as you deem necessary.

Plan a Few Conversations

Once people start attending and participating in your community, especially if you have some type of forum, the community will take on a life of its own. Community participation and community satisfaction are positively correlated, in that the more people post, the happier they will be with the community.[12] The more they visit and participate, the greater the trust they will have in the community and the store.

However, you will be able to direct the types of conversations that your online community will have. Consider the examples we have already provided, and think about the following type of conversations you can have on your board or on your blog.

Information Exchanges. Many communities will have some type of information exchange going on regularly. You will want to think about your social glue and develop a personalized focus on some specific areas that address what your customers/community members are most interested in. Let us say, for example, you own a vitamin store and your online community will focus on health. You should think what specific health information you want to focus on. Then set up specific conversational areas on your community forum or dedicate a blog posting to one specific area each day. There will be some information that you will want to provide, as you will have access to some information from your vendors that may be of interest to members in the community.

You will probably also want community members to be able to post information too, like the posts at the Kraft recipe exchange board. You should make sure, though, that the information that is not the intellectual property of the board members is properly credited to their authors to avoid any copyright issues. Also welcome members to post questions that will stimulate people to provide information that they know.

Rituals. A ritual is defined as a "stylized and meaningful sequence of actions that binds people more closely together."[13] Rituals are moments of belonging that define who we are and where we belong. Communities often have rituals, and you might want to think about some certain events that happen on a weekly or monthly basis that give some structure to the community and generate some type of response from lurkers and nonlurkers alike.

An example of this is a regularly scheduled poll. You could create a simple poll each week. Community members can respond and see how others can respond. For example, on a cooking board you could ask what the favorite type of Christmas cookie is. You might also want to consider having a monthly contest or drawing, where you randomly select a post from all the posts that have come in and give that person a prize. You could also consider a "post your photo" contest where people take pictures of themselves at your store or using your products. Members could vote on the best picture, and the person who took the picture wins a prize.

Product and Service Ratings. As we described earlier, you may want to offer product ratings and reviews of the items you sell in your store. This is also known as the eBay or Amazon model. Studies that have investigated situations where consumers share product reviews and purchase experiences have shown that others' experiences have a great influence on individuals, especially if the others are trusted.[14]

You need to be especially vigilant when people have issues or problems with the products or services they purchase at your store. Investigate all problems and correct any of the issues that you can. Be sure to let the community know what your response was.

Ask the Expert. Perhaps one of your community members is an expert in your social glue. Invite him or her to be a special guest to answer some questions posed by other members of the community. Alternatively, consider occasionally inviting an outside expert to join the community for a specific period of time for an ask the expert type of experience. The expert you invite should, of course, be related to your social glue. Some examples:

- Ask the Chef: invite a local chef to answer questions about food.
- Ask the Inventor: invite the inventor of a product that you sell.
- Ask the Child Development Expert: for communities devoted to kids.
- Ask the Pharmacist: for communities devoted to health or senior issues.

Also consider having you and members of your staff available for an Ask the Store section. Ideas for this section include:

- Ask the Owner: a place where people can have a direct line to you.
- Ask the Wait Person: invite a staff member to give answers to what service staff really think and experience.
- Ask the Stylist: if someone has just been to a training class, allow them to answer questions about new styles, products, and services.

Whatever you end up doing, you might want to think about occasional events to bring the online community face to face. We live most of our lives in the physical world, in the real world. There's nothing wrong with attempting to bridge these two worlds, and in fact, people are more likely to find an online community more meaningful if they feel they have the opportunity to meet someone in real life.[15]

TAKING IT FURTHER: FACILITATING AND MODERATING YOUR COMMUNITY

Like an in-store community, successful virtual communities are focused on the needs of community members, and put their goals and needs first, not the store's. Community members want information and connections; when they get what they want, they tell others about the community, and this will hopefully translate into visits and revenue for your store.

Online communities tend to be meritocracies in that those who have a high level of knowledge or expertise are likely to be respected and acknowledged by other members.[16] They play a key role in how your community evolves. Your virtual community will have informal leaders. Leaders are most clearly evident in forums where people are asking questions and looking for feedback and assistance from others in the community. Communities can fail if you do not engage such experts and keep them involved.

You might wish to consider inviting several key leaders to help you facilitate the conversations. You and the other facilitators keep the momentum of the community going by keeping the discussion directed in some way.

Other specific tasks of the facilitators are:

- To welcome new people to the group. Facilitators should help them introduce themselves to the community, and inform them of any group norms that have developed.
- To listen and respond regularly to the conversations happening on the Web. Facilitators should also keep you informed of the basic tone of the conversations online, and alert you to any conversations you need to be involved with.
- To keep the discussion lively. Facilitators should ask questions, suggest new paths for discussions, and probe for a greater depth of information. They should also introduce new topics that engage the members in meaningful conversations,
- To moderate activities that provide insights for your store. If facilitators notice that a key discussion is started, they should let you know as soon as possible so you can respond and act on the information.
- Related to this, good facilitators also observe patterns among the community and are able to postulate what these might mean to the company's business strategy.
- Whenever possible, your facilitators should stay neutral and suspend personal opinions as much as possible to instigate new conversations.

Once people start participating, they will feel like the site is theirs. You can set guidelines but you cannot be a big brother in control of everything that happens. Attempts for you to control the discussions will keep participants from freely discussing the information that is important to the site. Create guidelines, such as "do not say anything online that you would not say in person in our store." Your role as a moderator is to clarify anything that people have questions about your store but not to edit posts or to police the site. Think of your virtual community as a free speech area. Moderators should rarely delete the postings unless the postings are advertisements or personal attacks.[17]

TAKING IT FURTHER: MAKING THE THIRD PLACE

Your online community is likely to take on a life of its own. This is your ultimate goal: to have your community to be the third place in your customer's lives. To keep that third place a safe and meaningful place for your customers, you need to understand how the unique nature of the Internet affects this community. As you have probably figured out, online communities are very different animals from offline communities. Our best suggestions on maintaining this wonderful third place follow.

You will need a designated moderator. We have discussed how you and others will be facilitators of the online community. You (or someone you designate, perhaps an employee of your store) will also perform the role of the moderator—the owner and ultimate decision maker of the community. In addition to facilitating responsibilities, the role of the moderator is to:

- Manage the membership, including approving registrations.
- Being the technical expert, answering any general questions on how things work at the community.
- Marketing the list to others, promoting membership.
- Ensuring that flaming and other types of attacks are not present.

Indeed, the care and feeding of an online community can take a significant amount of time—perhaps two to three hours a week or more.

You will need to understand the role of lurkers in your community, and think about ways to involve them. As we mentioned earlier, about 10–30 percent of your community will be active at any time. The rest of the people, the ones not actively participating, are described as lurkers, those who observe what is going on and remain silent. Some of these lurkers may spend a lot of time on your site, and may closely follow the conversations of the community. They often feel closely tied to the community in spite of their lurking behavior.[18] Although they may not be active participants, their visiting the community may result in turning them into better customers.

Lurkers do not really harm the community, but they are clearly not active participants who are growing and participating in the community. Therefore, they get the benefits of the community without giving anything back. A study by Preece found several reasons why lurkers did not actively participate:

- They did not understand the community.
- They did not have the time to post.
- They did not feel a need to post. They could get the information they needed without asking for it; they were reading with a specific goal in mind.
- They felt safer not posting (in terms of privacy and the ability to offend someone).[19]

Following some of the instructions we have provided in this chapter will help overcome some of these obstacles. That is, make your site easy to use, indicate how you protect people's privacy, and make the motivations of the community clear. In addition, consider rewarding those people for contributing. You can give special discounts or enter them into a drawing. Do not make it a big deal, though, because you will just be encouraging them to interact even more. The idea is a simple signal to the lurkers that they can get back even more by giving to the community.

Be aware of how members manage identity in the online environment. Remember the old *New Yorker* cartoon of the dog at the computer, with the caption, "On the Internet, nobody knows you are a dog"? The Internet lacks traditional social markers that provide people with information about one another (i.e., visual cues of age, gender, and race). Thus, the Internet can lead to people adopting identities that are not their own.

In some cases, this is not necessarily a bad thing: if people feel more comfortable posting under a different persona than their own, and are contributing to the conversation in a positive or productive way, then it is not a big deal. However, there are a few instances that you should be aware of that can occur.

- *Trolls*: A troll is someone who attempts to pass as a legitimate member of the group. Initially a troll seems to be interested in the community's social glue. After a while, though, they begin to be disruptive in conversations, they disseminate bad information, and can hurt the feeling of trust that is developed in the community.[20] You, as a moderator, can ban the troll, although the best thing to do is not to engage anyone who demonstrates this behavior. A lack of attention will often cause them to leave the community and look for fun elsewhere.
- *Impersonators*: Another type of deception involves impersonation, where one individual adopts another's identity. It is relatively easy to say you are someone else online, since there are few identity cues. For example, someone could join the community saying they are a loyal shopper but are instead an owner of a competitive store. How harmful this is depends on the types of messages posted by the individual. If they violate the rules you have set up, ban them from the board. If they constantly downgrade your store and suggest members shop somewhere else, answer the accusations as best you can.

Consider actions when inevitable miscommunications occur. The social presence theory addresses how media convey a sense of the participants being physically present, using face-to-face communication as a standard for the assessment.

The Internet has the characteristic of having reduced social cues. Without visual and aural cues, such as facial expression, body language, and tone of voice, it is possible (and in fact sometimes simple) for messages to be misinterpreted, leading to frustrations, hurt feelings, and angry responses. Some people feel that they can behave more aggressively online because they are not in the physical presence of others in the community.

How do you address this? You can provide ways to increase social presence, such as allowing community members to post photographs or icons to represent themselves. Additionally, many communities recommend the use of "linguistic softeners" to avoid being thought as aggressive. For example, people may start a comment with the phrase "IMHO," meaning "in my humble opinion," as a way to soften any strong language. You might also consider using a hosting forum that allows participants to post a personal profile, so subscribers can reveal more about themselves as they choose so others can get to know them a bit better. This may moderate some communication issues always inherent in online conversations, which lack subtleties of voice and facial expressions that can provide so much to personal interaction.

Think about using online and in-store communities together. Should you try to arrange for online community to meet IRL (in real life)? Absolutely! Studies show that people are more open and honest if the opportunity to meet online community members in real life can occur. Once people meet and make connections with each other, there's a good chance that they will set up something like this on their own. However, you can facilitate an event that can get them in your store, such as the following:

- Special shopping night: have one night a month when the store is open only to community members. They will come to shop and to meet the people they talk with online. Consider offering some type of special discount or promotional offer for these customers at that time.
- Have a small button printed that customers can wear on their lapels when they are at your store. Then, they can identify other community members when they are shopping. Think about offering some type of special whenever someone wears a button when shopping.
- Have an in-store community bulletin board where online community members can put pictures of themselves, so those visiting the store will be able to recognize them when they see them. Have a drawing once a month for people who put their pictures up.

SUMMING UP

In this chapter, we have shown you:

- The specific benefits of online communities.
- The difference between forums, blogs, and social networking sites.
- The steps you need to take to start your online community.
- The role of moderators, lurkers, experts, and other community members.
- Some of the pitfalls you might run into in an online community and how to deal with them.

The most important thing for you to consider is your social glue: What will bond the people in your community together to make them active and interested participants? Thinking about your social glue, reviewing your research, talking to customers and staff will likely result in some interesting ideas for your social glue.

In the next chapter, we will go into more detail on your real-life community and how the two can be linked for maximum results.

RESOURCE TOOLBOX

Many services provide ready-to-go message boards and forum templates and software. For example:

- groups.yahoo.com (you will need a free Yahoo! account)
- forum.snitz.com
- www.vbulletin.com

There are also several services that provide blogging capabilities. Look into:

- www.blogger.com
- www.typepad.com
- www.movabletype.org
- www.livejournal.com

For a summary of how the different blog services compare, read the article found at http://www.sitepoint.com/article/blog-software-smackdown-review.

Social networking sites:

- www.myspace.com
- www.facebook.com
- www.friendster.com

Chapter **7**

Growing and Supporting Your Online Community

Customers → Conversations → Community → *Commitment*

Your online community should be the central focus of your community-building efforts. In addition, there are other ways to add to your community efforts that will enhance your business. The goal of these types of additional programs is to give you, members of your staff, and members of your community the opportunity to interact with your community face to face. As we mentioned in the previous chapter, people are more likely to be involved in online communities if they have the opportunity to meet community members. We see three different ways that you can support and enhance your online community.

1. *An in-store community.* You have some type of program in your store that gets community members off their computers and into your store so they meet other members and can purchase what you have to sell.
2. *An employee community.* Involve your employees in both your online and in-store efforts so that your sales staff will be able to meet the members of your community and get to know them on a different level.
3. *An outreach community.* Become involved in an issue, a cause, or a charity organization that is of interest to you, to members of your online community, and to your employees to strengthen that sense of commitment to the community from all your community members.

In this chapter, we will talk about each of these support communities individually. If you do not know which of these support communities is best for you, read about each of the communities and then make a decision. If you already have an idea of a group or cause that you would like to get involved with, or if you are already involved with a specific group on a charitable basis, focus on that specific section of this chapter.

GETTING STARTED: WAYS TO GET ONLINE MEMBERS INTO YOUR STORE

You have created your online community, and by now you should have a pretty good idea of what the social glue that holds your community together has become. Understanding this social glue will help you in formulating a plan for your in-store community. Once you know your social glue, proceed through the following steps to make decisions about your in-store community.

Connect Your Store Environment to Your Social Glue

Perhaps you have noticed that your social glue is based around a demographic similarity of the people in your community: The people online talking to each other are similar in age, in gender, in ethnicity. Armed with this knowledge, take a walk around your store and look at it through the eyes of the specific group of people you want to bring in to see if you can make some physical alterations to make your store more appealing to this group. This might involve changing some of the space in your store to appeal to community members and/or adding some products or services that appeal specifically to these groups.

Parents and kids: Let us say you created an online community for parents and you want to make a place in your store for both parents and kids to come and spend time together. This is a great strategy, since children have an amazing amount of disposable income: Recent statistics show that the average kid controls $3,500 to $4,000 per year. Additionally, children are strong influencers on their parents; they encourage them to visit stores that appeal to both the parents and the kids. Look around and see what you currently offer, and see what you have that can be of interest to kids. If parents bring their kids to the store, and they are likely to meet more parents with kids, then they will naturally start to talk and meet. Here are some ideas of how to be more kid-friendly.

If you are a:	*Think about offering:*
Beauty salon	Special services that might appeal to kids, such as nonpermanent hair color.
Restaurant	Kids' menu with special items.
Camera store	A special area where kids can play with a used Polaroid camera and keep the photographs.

| Hardware store | A "kids corral" where kids can play with plastic tools and construction toys. |
| Card and gift store | A kids' table with crayons and paper for kids to make their own cards. |

If you are going to create a parents/kids community, develop a kids' area for your store. For instance, lower items to kids' eye level, have a seating area of kids chairs, etc. In addition, think about having activities for kids to do in the store. Have a video area with a brightly colored rug for kids to sit on, a toy box with appropriate toys, or a chalkboard where kids can be occupied while parents shop or while they are waiting to receive a service.

Senior community: What if you have created an online community for seniors? As you might have noticed, the senior market is huge and growing at a constant rate. More than one-third of all adults are aged fifty. Over the next ten or fifteen years, the number of Americans aged fifty-plus will total more than 115 million. At the same time, the number of people aged eighteen to thirty-four will decrease by about 5 percent. Seniors age fifty and over own 80 percent of financial assets in the United States and control 50 percent of disposable income. At the same time, only about 10 percent of advertising messages are directed to them. The myth that seniors are not adventurous consumers is just that—a myth. Today's seniors are perceptive consumers who are as interested in new products and services as their younger consumer counterparts are. They have more time and seek destinations where they can interact and engage with others. They are value conscious, but they are also quality conscious. They also tend to be loyal to retailers that service them well.

Do you offer products that will be attractive to seniors? Seniors are often looking for smaller meals at restaurants and single serving or smaller sized products at retail shops. Consider whether it is possible to repackage existing offerings to make them appealing to seniors. Once seniors decide to become customers, they are often highly loyal. Additionally, seniors often travel in groups and pass on information to others in the senior community. Here are some other ideas on ways to be senior-friendly.

If you are a:	*Think about offering:*
Bookstore	A special book club just for seniors.
Restaurant	"Senior Table" where seniors on their own can share a meal with other seniors; smaller senior meals and meal packages.
Shoe store	More comfortable chairs reserved for seniors to try on shoes.
Florist	Classes for seniors in plant care.
Gym	Seniors-only exercise classes.

Multicultural communities: Do you have a large number of multicultural customers? If so, one thing to think about as you walk around your store is whether your signage is appropriate or whether you need to use the community-dominant language in addition to English in your store. Your decision will depend on your multicultural customers and what language they tend to use. Visit other establishments in the neighborhood and see what they do. If you notice a trend toward community-dominant language, consider adding it to your in-store signs.

If you choose to use the community-dominant language, remember to not simply translate the words to the language, but keep in mind idioms and other language idiosyncrasies. Think about hiring a local speaker of the community-dominant language to help craft your advertising messages and to work with the staff at your store.

Display a welcome sign in the community-dominant language to invite customers into the store. Think about in-store signs in the community-dominant language also. Learning how to verbally greet people in a language other than English is a positive gesture, as is having bilingual employees. Think about hiring bilingual employees who can extend the welcome in the community-dominant language. If you do have multicultural customers, investigate adding some products or services that might appeal specifically to them. Here are some more thoughts on multicultural marketing.

If you are a:	*Think about offering:*
Clothing store	Girlfriend shopping afternoon or night with refreshments.
Deli	Revolving specials relating to the community's interests and holidays.
Sporting goods store	A greater range of equipment popular among multicultural audiences; show games on television and invite customers to join you to watch the event.
Video rental store/bar or tavern	Special sections of multicultural films; sponsor viewing parties at a bar or tavern.

College-student community: If you live in a university town, think of connecting with the university in some way. College students may not be big spenders, but they tend to be very loyal to places that welcome them. In one university town, for example, a new pub opened on the other side of campus from the popular campus bars. The pub invited different faculty members to hold their evening classes or to have a special lecture at their pub on the slow nights. This regular gathering became a way for several dozen students to try a new restaurant (most of the students ended up ordering a drink and/or an appetizer) and making them feel comfortable at the pub. The pub then created a unique niche for themselves as a center for intellectual chat rather than a party-crazy bar like the other ones on campus.

Create Activities Related to the Social Glue

Your social glue might not be demographic-based; instead, it might be based on interests and lifestyles of members of the community. This type of social glue gives you a springboard to think about activities that will be of interest to members of your community. Activities are the heart of your community. They give people a reason to become a regular participant in the group. In some ways, activities are the community rituals. Rituals are a social process where the meaning of the community is reinforced within the community. The rituals are a key element of the social glue. Activities often begin around consumption experiences, but eventually, as the community starts to develop, the group will determine the types of activities they are most interested in.

Initially, though, you should come up with a regular slate of activities or meetings for your community. Depending on the type of community, these can be highly structured, largely informal, or somewhere in between. When you are starting out, think about a mix of formal and informal activities. A formal activity would be seen as some type of educational presentation that would allow your community members to meet each other and learn something new. An informal activity would not have a structured information component, but would allow a natural gathering with information and support exchanged between members of the community.

The type of structure will depend on the nature of the social glue and the amount of effort you are willing to put into the initial stages of building the community. For example, if you are starting a monthly gourmet night at your restaurant, you will need to arrange for the table, create the menu, check on the RSVPs, and act as the host during the meals. If you are going to have a drop-in scrapbooking night at the big table in the store, then you will not have to do much more about it after you have invited people and they have indicated their interest.

The amount of space will determine the type of activities you can host in your store; combine this with the idea of the social glue that your online community is built around and you will come up with some good ideas on how to structure your online community.

MOVING FORWARD: CREATING A COMMUNITY SPACE IN YOUR STORE

It is important to have some type of physical space for your in-store community. If you have enough space, you will want to create some type of central hub in your store: We call this the dining room table idea. This could be a table in the middle or off to the side of your store, or even in a small separate room like a classroom. The table should comfortably hold six or eight people, so people know that it is a place for gathering and talking. The best example of this that you will see is at a yarn store. Many yarn stores have tables where customers gather for classes or just to drop in and knit. While in the store, they get help and encouragement from the staff and from other knitters. The shop becomes a gathering place, and the nature of this third place will cause people to spend more time in the store than before.

Action Idea: Take a walk around your store and see what you might be able to move around in order to create a community space for your customers and employees. Do not be afraid to reconfigure some aspect of your store to create this space.

When you first set up the table, you might need to put a table tent explaining its purpose: "Our new wine appreciation (or holiday decorating or Steiff bear collector) group will be meeting here soon. Let us know if you'd like to come." Here are more ideas.

If you are a:	*Think about offering:*
Craft store	Craft table.
Restaurant	Gourmet table, hors d'oeuvres table, tasting table with a specific theme.
Photography store	Scrapbooking table.
Hardware store	Table with decorating books.
Computer store	Test drive table with computers where guests can try out new programs.

Even stores that do not have a table could organize a regular group activity that would allow people to meet at the store and get to know others. As mentioned, a sporting goods store could organize a running or walking group, as well as be the meeting point for other related excursions (meet at the store to carpool to a ski resort or to a hike, for example). Many other types of stores can lend themselves to outside experiences. A pet supply store, for example, could sponsor a weekly pet walk where pet owners could meet each other while walking their pets. A garden store could sponsor a regular garden amble where participants walk through different neighborhoods or parks to look at gardens. A food store could sponsor a trip to a street fair to sample a range of different foods. Auto parts stores could sponsor trips to car expos. The list is endless, but just for starters, check out the following options.

If you are a:	*Think about sponsoring:*
Camera store	Photography walk where leader helps group members take pictures.
Sporting goods store	Running/walking groups; trips to ski resorts.
Pet store	Pet walk.
Garden store	Garden amble where people visit different neighborhoods or parks.
Auto parts store	Trip to car expo.

Another physical sign that shows that you have a community is the presence of a dedicated community bulletin board. Make sure that it is clear that the bulletin board is not a general interest board. (Monitor the board to make sure this happens. You certainly want to be accommodating to the local high school drama club, but their poster can go somewhere else, not on your community bulletin board.) On the bulletin board, you will want to include the next time the community will gather, notes from the last gathering, contact information, pictures, articles, and any type of information that may be of interest to members of your community. Of course, you should also include this information on your Web site and tell interested people how to become part of the community.

As a complement to the out-of-store event, think about offering a formal in-store activity that will be of interest based around the out-of-store event (see Table 7-1). For your running group or for other sports groups that meet at your store and then go off somewhere else, offer nutritional workshops or seminars on training for a marathon. The key is to extend the social glue in meaningful ways that will encourage customer conversations.

Regardless of the type of activity that you offer, think about providing some type of special offer before, during, or after the community activities. Example: 10 percent off all purchases while the community is meeting.

Here are some thoughts on the types of activities you could offer initially. What is important to remember, though, is that your community needs to regularly gather to interact with each other. Keep in mind that eventually the community will gel together to establish their own ideas on the types of things they want to do.

Learning activities: For some communities, the formal activity will be easy to organize and implement. We discussed in the previous section some of the learning activities that can mesh with some of the other activities that you are going to sponsor. Most communities will be open to learning new things about their interests, and many people are more than happy (and extremely flattered) to be asked to come in and talk about their area of interest.

Table 7-1 In-Store Events that Complement Out-of-Store Events

If you are a	And your out-of-store event is	Think about offering
Camera store	Photography walk where leader helps group members take pictures	Seminar on digital darkrooms
Sporting goods store	Running/walking groups; trips to ski resorts	Slide show given of someone's ski trip
Pet store	Pet walk	Seminar on pet health
Garden store	Garden amble where people visit different neighborhoods or parks	Lecture by a local expert on native plants
Auto parts store	Trip to car expo	Talk by a representative of some of the new models seen at the show

If you are a:	Think about offering:
Auto parts store	Presentation on vintage Mustang convertibles or some other type of classic car.
Kitchen or housewares store	Product demonstration for some of the new products that you offer.
Garden store	Transplanting plants workshop.
Hardware store	Seminar on cabinet building.
Computer store	Test drive table with computers where guests can try out new programs under the tutelage of an employee.

Another tactic is to sponsor an information event: an on-site event that provides information. For example you could sponsor events for seniors about a topic that is of interest to them—health, nutrition, exercise, volunteering, or gardening—and then offer specials on the products they need to complete the activity.

Participation activities: Balance these formal events with more informal gatherings. For people whose interests are portable (like many crafts), providing an informal gathering on a regular basis is a great community-builder.

If you are a:	Think about offering:
Restaurant	Drop-in dessert table.
Kitchen or housewares store	Hands-on experimenting with new products and ingredients.
Bar or tavern	Sunday afternoon board game events.

Hardware store	Tool tune-up.
Card and gift store	Coloring books.

Ritual events: You might also think about establishing events based around established milestones, holidays, and rituals. For example, think about some formal events that celebrate milestones in a family's life. For example, have a graduation celebration in which you provide free cupcakes for kindergarten graduates and reduced prices on diploma frames. Focus on those aspects in your advertising. Think about other rituals (have one day per month to celebrate all October birthdays, for example) during otherwise slow periods. You can give discounts for kids' products that parents can use and that kids will like.

If you are a:	*Think about celebrating:*
Auto parts store	Indy 500 or other car races.
Office supply store	Back to school: balloons, contests for kids, and the like.
Garden store	Arbor Day, Earth Day.
Optical store	National vision care month.

Remember: always refer back to your social glue for a reality check on the decisions that you make.

MOVING FORWARD: INVOLVING YOUR EMPLOYEES IN COMMUNITY EFFORTS

We all know how important your employees are. They are responsible for the day-to-day running of your business, and you count on them to represent you to the public. The retail environment is especially competitive for recruiting and retaining good employees. The good news is that your efforts in developing a community can help you in developing loyal and satisfied employees. The more loyal your employees are, the more you can expect your customers to be more loyal and satisfied. Many employee studies have indicated that in addition to compensation, rewards and recognition are key drivers of their happiness at work. The community, then, can be a way to recognize their achievements and reward them for their work.

> **Action Idea:** Schedule a special staff meeting where the topic is the social glue of the community. Share your thoughts, but also be open to the ideas of your employees.

- *Involve employees in decisions about the community.* As you start to create and assess the social glue that holds your community together, keep your employees involved and informed. Consider their own interests and expertise when you think about your social glue. This will help them become committed to the programs that you implement.
- *Invite and encourage employees to join the community.* If you are developing in-store activities, ask your employees to consider taking a role in the activities, either as a leader or as a participant. See if they are interested in creating or leading some type of workshop or information session, or organizing an outside activity that meets at the store. Some employees will naturally gravitate to leadership positions, others may feel more comfortable behind the scenes (doing things such as organizing the bulletin board, working on the Web site, and other hands-on activities that need attention to detail). Including your employees in the community will reinforce that they are an important part of the store's team. By doing so, you will increase their teamwork skills, their morale, and their overall trust in the organization. It will also help to develop their respect for diversity and their understanding of others not quite like them.
- *Assign employees to facilitate certain activities.* If you have included them in some of your key decisions about your social glue, it is likely that your employees are going to be open, and even eager, to become part of your online community. You can strengthen this commitment by asking them to facilitate some of the activities in your community. For example, give them access to information that might help others in the community. Consider making them responsible for information on how to fix or repair items, or on what types of new items have been ordered for the store.
- *Use employees as your eyes and ears.* Another way to get them involved in your online community is to rely on your employees to help you debrief and make sense of what the people in the community are talking about. Schedule regular sessions during staff meetings to hear these employee debriefs and to recognize the importance of learning this information. With (hopefully) many great conversations going on, you might miss a key discussion here or there that can help you understand more about your customer base and the things you need to do that will make your store even more successful. Ask your employees what their take-away from both in-store and online activities is. What are the hot topics that people are talking about? What is on their minds? What is upsetting them? Then take this information and see if there is something you can do in your store to address these issues. Your employees might also have some innovative ideas on how to address these issues. Keeping these channels of communication open with your employees will help you keep your finger on the pulse of the activity of your community. This will enhance communication and organization skills, as well as communication skills.

MOVING FORWARD: ROLES YOUR EMPLOYEES CAN PLAY

The success of a community lies in its leadership, and once you start to build the community it will be good for you to step back and let others take over. You can do this simply by looking around at the membership and seeing who might be a good person to take over, based on his or her interest and connection to the community as well as the strength of his or her relationships with others in the community. Your employees might be great choices to be leaders: Ask them whether they'd be interested in introducing a speaker, starting a discussion, leading a trip. You may have several employees who are willing to take on the leadership role. Even if you do not, you can let your employees know who the community leaders are and encourage them to develop relationships with them. You might also ask your employees to host an in-store event or to be a designated greeter for one of your events.

Employee leadership is extremely valuable. What is most important in your community leadership is that your employee leaders can generate passion for the community. If you include your employees in decision making, they are likely to become passionate about your community. Research has shown that in 80 percent of cases, the leading voices make a community vibrant. Your employees are involved in the store for many hours a week, and will hopefully take the passion from the community into the store . . . and then take that passion for the store back to the online community.

Another role of the employee leaders will be to nurture the newer people in the community. One of the greatest challenges to any type of community is the fear of not belonging. People who do not think they will fit into a community are likely to see this as a barrier to participation. If your employees have the responsibility of making people feel welcome to the online community, to make them feel at home, and to see what they need to maintain their involvement with the community, you will know that this area is always being covered.

It can be easy to let your community evolve into a clique that does not want to let anyone else in. Ask your employees to discourage this whenever you see that happening. Model welcoming behavior for your leaders, and they will pick up on it and see that as a key value to your community. Asking your employees to take on these roles is giving them a task that is different from others in the community. It is also a way to recognize and reward them, which are key things you need to do in order to keep the community humming along and to keep your employees happy and satisfied.

TAKING IT FURTHER: REACHING OUT TO LOCAL ORGANIZATIONS TO AID YOUR COMMUNITY EFFORTS

Hosting in-store activities may not be the best fit for your store. You may not have enough space to comfortably host a gathering of customers. You may not have a social glue that lends itself to in-store activities. You may simply not want people hanging out in your store (if you own a jewelry store, or sell some other high-end good, it is quite likely that an in-store community may not work well for you). In lieu of in-store communities, think about outreach communities—that is, becoming a force in a local community group. For stores that do not have a distinct specialty around which a community could be built, consider reaching out to the community at large and using an existing community to help build a community in your store. This allows you to tap into an existing community that is likely to need some type of help and support.

It is also another way to build customer loyalty. Today's consumers are conscious about shopping at local stores in their neighborhood that are actively involved in their community. They expect retailers to give back to the community. A certain portion of customers view this as a key differentiating feature in what stores they visit. This can be a highly effective method that contributes to building a positive image for the business while helping a deserving group gain much-needed visibility. In today's tough competitive environment, American consumers consistently demonstrate that a company's support for an important cause plays a critical role in their purchasing decisions. In fact, 76 percent of Americans have switched brands and/or retailers when their purchase benefited a cause they viewed as important. Additionally, two-thirds of consumers have greater trust in companies aligned with some type of community or social group or cause.

There are several simple steps that you should follow in order to build an outreach community.

- *Select a cause or a group to affiliate with.* First, think about whether there is a specific group that you and your employees are interested in. Do you love the opera, the local theater group, or the minor league baseball team? Why not connect with these groups and work on something with them? It is a different kind of social glue, but it is a glue all the same.
- *Find out what groups are in your trading area.* Think about proximity to your store. Go back to the map that you developed in Chapter 2 and see not only what organizations are in your trading area but also where people who volunteer at different organizations live. Whenever possible, you will want to keep things in the neighborhood to take advantage of the importance of

Action Idea: Put together a list of activities that are popular in your area. Many community groups are built around activities that kids are involved in from the major schools to sports and activities. Examples include AYSO, Little League, kids theater and chorus groups, and the like. Many communities have cultural centers that organize events around special days like Cinco De Mayo and the Asian New Year. Additionally, local churches and schools may have special programs that need sponsorships, fundraising, and a place to be able to talk about their community.

proximity to your store. Determine which activities have the largest enroll-
ment and thus the greatest reach among potential customers. Match these
activities to the social glue you have established in your online community,
and you probably have the potential for a successful partnership!

- ***Pick one or two groups.*** It is better for you to establish ongoing relationships
  with one or two community organizations, rather than working with as
  many as possible. Try to establish relationships that are fundraising efforts
  rather than straight donations to organizations. Both you and the organization will get more out of a fundraising effort. Use your online members, especially your Store Champions, to help you evaluate which groups to select.
- ***Talk to people at the organization.*** Contact the organizers of these groups;
  talk to the organizers at churches, schools, and cultural centers; and see
  how your store can help them achieve their goals. Building relationships
  with the managers and staff at these organizations will give you a chance to
  get to know them and most important, give them a chance to get to know
  you and your store. These people are going to be effective in delivering
  word-of-mouth messages to their friends and family, so make sure they are
  knowledgeable and satisfied with your store. You might want to think about
  offering a discount to these managers and personnel on a one-time basis to
  sample your store, so they can tell others more about it. If you have a service business, think about a free service to employees (such as a complimentary uniform dry cleaning or a manicure). The stronger your relationship
  with the managers, the stronger your outreach community will be.
- ***Negotiate your affiliation.*** Additionally, you will want to talk about the pa-
  rameters of your partnership. Will it be event-based (i.e., sponsorship of
  one or two events a year)? Will you offer some type of discount to members
  of the organization, or give a monetary donation based on the amount of
  products or services purchased? Will you give gifts in kind (i.e., donate
  products or employee time for the organization)?

TAKING IT FURTHER: SELECTING ACTIVITIES

What types of activities you select will depend on the organization's needs and
your own interests. Here are a few ideas for you to consider.

- ***Fundraising.*** There are many different ways to work with the organization
  on a fundraising activity. For example, you can promote the group's
  fundraising activity at your store (through posters on the windows) and in
  the other communications you send out to your mailing lists. Give the
  group some space outside your store if they wish to set up a bake sale or
  some other sidewalk-type fundraising event or sell tickets to the group's
  garden walk or holiday showcase. You might even consider hosting planning meetings for the fundraiser in your store after hours.

- *Provide some level of sponsorship at events run by the organization.* Set up a table at a cultural event or a community program sponsored by the organization. You might want to provide some information for the particular community reached by the organization or develop some other type of reference that could be distributed at the table. If you are working with an animal shelter, for example, produce a brochure about how to bathe your pet (use the Google search engine to search for "how to bathe your pet" if you need more information, or work with the organization to develop that information). Be sure to include your store's name on all publicity for the event. If you are sponsoring a kids' sports team, put your store's name on the team shirts and put up pictures of the team at your store.
- *Sell products that would be of interest to members of the group.* A drug store sold collector's edition cancer-themed stamps, mounted and framed in a uniquely designed display. This is a great holiday idea for collectors, cancer survivors, or anyone who wants to support cancer research and care. Proceeds from sales benefited the Hope Cancer Fund. Ask the leadership of the organization what types of products or services would be of interest to them and to people who have an affinity with the organization. Use this input to develop the promotion.
- *Give a small percent of sales on certain days to the group.* Donate a small percentage on sales of specific products (or products throughout the store) to the group. Promote this at the store and have the specific community promote it also.
- *Provide supporters with a discount at your store.* Give people who are members or donors of the organization a discount, either with every purchase or at specific times of the year. A Pittsburgh eyewear shop, Eyetique, raises funds for local cancer initiatives through designers' trunk shows and events for cancer research and patient care. Patrons who mention the Cancer Center receive a 20 percent discount on eyewear at the store.
- *Provide a free service to group members.* If you provide a service, select a specific day and offer free services to members of a group to get them to sample your store. This does not have to be a high-cost service—just enough to get them in the door. Here are some examples.

If your store is:	Think about donating:
A beauty salon	A manicure.
A video rental store	A one-night rental.
A dry cleaners or laundry	Dry cleaning of a sweater.
An automotive repair store	A trip check or tire rotation.

- *Donate services to support the organization.* A twist on the free service is to connect it directly with donations to the organization. For example, a laundry service in Cincinnati (called Appearance Plus) sponsors a Coats for Kids Campaign where they dry-cleaned coats and blankets for free that were then distributed to the needy. This got people in the store, and the store estimated that the cost of customer acquisition dropped from $150 to $50 per customer.

TAKING IT FURTHER: SUCCESSFULLY IMPLEMENTING COMMUNITY MARKETING PROGRAMS

You have thought about some causes or groups that you'd like to help out, you thought about some ways you could help them, and you are ready to get started. Here are some final thoughts on how to make the most of your program.

- *Clarify and confirm the details with the group.* Be sure that all parties understand your level of participation and commitment to the group and also confirm the group's role in the partnership. There's a range of possible marketing benefits from working with groups, and the organizers need to understand that this type of relationship should be a win-win situation for all. Some specific things to consider: how visible will your name be at events and at the community group's location and Web site? Be specific about what you expect. Spell out the details and then, if possible, get a signed contract.
- *Promote the events you participate in.* Think about ways you can get attention to the events and to your store's participation. You should also seek local media coverage. Call the local television and radio stations and ask if they'd be interested in covering the event. Send out emails to your email list to let people know of your participation and ultimately of the program's success. You will constantly be asked for donations. By affiliating with only a few groups, you will have a graceful way to decline all these extra donation requests.
- *Measure results.* We will talk more about measurement in an upcoming chapter, but think about a way to put metrics on the process to measure your results so you can learn what works and what does not. You can request a periodic report, as informal as you like, from the organization to get their input on how your partnership has affected their goals. Alternatively, assign an employee to track sales or promotions, preferably someone who cares about the alliance.
- *Get employees involved.* It makes good business sense to include your employees in some of the decisions you have made about your outreach community. Check in with them to see how they are feeling about the relationship. Working with an outreach community should give them a strong sense of satisfaction and purpose, and you will want to make sure that they are pleased with how the relationship is going.

- *Finally, be sure you continue to care about the issue.* Having a genuine passion or interest in the cause means that you and your employees will stay engaged with the group and you will still feel successful even if marketing efforts fall a tad short. If you do not have this passion, people will be able to tell, and this can hurt the credibility of your company.

SUMMING UP

In this chapter, we have shown you how to:

- Set up an in-store community to complement your online community.
- Get your employees involved.
- Collaborate with charitable organizations to create a win-win community situation.

Complementing your online community with opportunities for members to meet face to face is a great way to build momentum for your store. It also allows you to make personal connections with your customers. But how will it affect your bottom line? We will review that in the next chapter.

Chapter **8**

Tracking the Results

Customers → Conversations → Community → *Commitment*

Supporting your online community with in-store, employee, and outreach marketing are all strong and important ways to show your commitment to your innovative use of marketing techniques. The Getting Started section talks about the philosophy of measuring your success by implementing some tracking and measurement programs that will help you understand how each of your efforts is working. The Moving Forward section provides a range of ideas on tracking your efforts. These metrics will provide you with information that will help you tweak and refine your programs, will help you decide which programs to keep and which to stop, and will provide benchmarks for future activities. The Taking It Further section talks about sharing this information with your loyal customers and your employees. This will help them understand how individual efforts contribute to the success of the business—and of their community—as a whole.

GETTING STARTED: DEFINING SUCCESS AND TRACKING RESULTS

Your first step is to define for yourself what your idea of success is. The main measure of success will be some increase in overall sales and/or profits. However, we encourage you to add other forms of measurement to your definition of success. Is it an increase in employee retention rates? Is it more traffic during slow times of your store? Are your customers happier? Do you see your Store Champions more frequently, and are you meeting the people that they've referred to your store?

Also think about your success by noticing how things change over time. Remember, unlike a coupon or some other type of money off deal, the programs we discuss in this book will take a while to take hold among customers. Therefore, it'll take a bit longer to be able to see some measurable successes on your end, regardless of your measurement metric. So we encourage you to measure quarterly: after three months, six months, nine months, a year, so you can see how the gradual build-up of change is happening in your organization.

Defining your success is also a way to increase your commitment to the program. We know you will want to check the changes in your bottom line. But you should also be aware of other changes that are more difficult to quantitatively measure, such as if you see employees happier in their jobs, customers taking the time to stop and chat with you on a regular basis, more referrals and more people telling you that they are making referrals. These show that your efforts are working and having a positive impact on your community of employees and customers. Continuing the dialogue with customers will also give you ideas of what is not working, so you can change or alter these plans and get on track. All of these events will also eventually have a very meaningful impact on your bottom line.

MOVING FORWARD: SALES MEASUREMENTS THAT TRACK CHANGES IN YOUR BUSINESS

The next step is to determine what and how to measure. There are many ways that a business can measure whether the programs you have selected are successful. Use these examples as guides. You may find other measurements that are slightly different than the ones listed that work better for you. The key is to have indicators that you look at regularly to help you determine whether or not your business is succeeding, stagnating, or declining. Some of the formulae we provide involve simple counts, some involve a little bit of math. A few involve intuitively assessing what's happening with your community. Think about what you have access to when deciding which formulae to use for tracking purposes.

Sales measurements use your sales figures to track changes in your business. Here are some key metrics for sales measurements.

Overall Customer/Guest Count Growth

Measuring changes (that is, increases) in the number of guests or customers that walk through your doors is easily the most significant sign of success. You will start with a benchmark: Measure the number of customers that come in during one week, and call that week one. This is your baseline from which you will do your measurements for the first month. Use the first week of each month as your week one in order to track growth during the month. If your business is not growing each week or each month in terms of the number of customers or guests that visit your store, then your store is stagnating. Keep in mind that you want this growth to be consistent and steady; do not worry if the growth is not extremely rapid. If your guest count grows too quickly, you may not be able to service the guests properly. This may indicate that you are too busy, and therefore your guests have a bad experience and will not return. Therefore, a gradual growth in guest count is ideally what you want. Continue comparing this information on a weekly basis so you learn about and take into consideration any seasonal fluctuations.

> *Formula*: Week 2 Guests – Week 1 Guests = Growth in number of guests
> Week 2 Guests/Week 1 Guests = Guest change rate

(Substitute subsequent weeks for week 2 as the year progresses.)
Example: During week 1 you had 200 guests. During week 2, you had 220 guests.

> Growth in number of guests = 220 – 200 = 20 new guests
> Guest change = 220/200 = 1.1 = 110% or a 10% growth in guests

For service businesses, you will be able to count the number of guests/customers that walk through your doors very easily, since practically every customer is going to result in a sale. For other businesses, though, you may have an increase in store traffic where people walk in but may not necessarily purchase anything. This is not necessarily a bad thing, since they may be shopping around and could come back later. You might want to provide your employees who are working the sales desk with a clicker or some other type of tallying mechanism so they can measure the total number of people who visit the store, regardless of whether they purchase anything. Your POS system can track the number of customers who actually purchase something. These numbers together will give you the best picture of what is happening at your store.

Repeat Guest Count Growth

Repeat guest count, which refers to the number of guests revisiting your business, is almost as important as sheer guest count growth. Why is this important? Because an increasing number of repeat guests is a clear sign of the quality of experience that you are providing in your store or business. What is a measurement of success? The right number depends on how often customers visit your store. For instance, a dry cleaner may have a frequency of visits every week or every other week. A restaurant may have a frequency of visit of once per month. A good rule of thumb is that the repeat guest percentage increases as overall percentage of total guests. For instance, as your guest count grows, your percentage of repeat guests may climb from 70 percent to 80 percent. This is a very good indicator of customer loyalty and demonstrates that a good service experience is happening in your business.

> *Formula*: Repeat Guests/Total Guests = Percentage of repeat guests

Example: During week 1 you have 100 repeat guests and 180 total guests. During week 5, you counted 200 repeat guests and 240 total guests.

Week 1: 100 Repeat Guests/180 Total Guests = 56% repeat guests
Week 5: 200 Repeat Guests/240 Total Guests = 83% repeat guests

If you have some type of loyalty program, you will easily be able to tell if someone has purchased from your store before. Additionally, your salespeople will probably be able to recognize many of your new customers from your repeat customers. Even so, have your salespeople keep a tally of the customers who are new and who are repeat at the checkout register to help you measure growth in repeat customers.

Upselling of Services or Products

This metric assesses the change in the number of services that your guests add on to their original request. Another way to describe this would be the number of items that you were able to upsell. For example, if someone comes into a salon for a haircut, did they add on a manicure or schedule a coloring? Other examples include ordering desserts in a restaurant or adding accessories in a clothing store. In either case, your guest is demonstrating how trusting they are in you and how loyal they are to your business. Guests come to stores on a regular basis to get basic items. When it becomes easier for you to approach them or sell them add-on services or accessories, this is an indication of increasing trust in you and your employees.

Formula: # Upsell items Week 2 – # of Upsell Items Week 1 = Upsell growth

$$\frac{\text{Upsell items Week 2}}{\text{Upsell items Week 1}} = \frac{\text{Rate of growth}}{\text{in upsell items}}$$

Example: You sell thirty desserts during week 1, and thirty-five during week 2.

35 – 30 = 5 Upsell growth
35/30 = 1.16 = 16% increase in upsell items

You will also want to look at the upsell percentage of overall customers. If your customer count is growing, make sure that your percentage of upsells as a percentage of customers is also growing. Again, keep track of this weekly to chart your success.

Increase in Number of Highest-Cost Products and Services

The next sign of success: Sales of your highest-cost (to you) product or service should be increasing. This is usually your most expensive product or service. If your highest-cost product or service is increasing, it demonstrates that your guests have added trust in your business. They are now comfortable with your store and are willing to select more expensive items to purchase. For instance, in the food service business, they might select higher-priced meat, or a full meal that includes dessert. In a dry cleaning business, they may select more trusted services such as cleaning for coats or suede jackets. At a bookstore, they might purchase more nonbook gift items like gourmet foods or coffees. Tally the purchase of these individual higher-cost items and compare these purchases to the frequency of purchase of the items in the past year or six months.

Sales Volume Growth

Every business must focus on how many dollars come into the store on a regular basis. You cannot pay the bills unless you have dollars coming in the door. Sales growth may be the ultimate sign of success. Note that sales volume growth can be misinterpreted. If sales are going up while costs are increasing at a higher rate, you're in trouble. Also, your sales volume can go up while your guest count is going down. Increases in your ticket average from upselling or price increases can mask stagnation in other areas. So do not rely on just bottom line sales growth.

Formula: Week 2 Sales – Week 1 Sales = Sales Growth
Week 2 Sales/Week 1 Sales = Rate of Growth in Sales

Example: Your sales during week 1 were $7000, and your sales during week 2 were $8800.

8800 – 7000 = 1800 increase in sales
8800/7000 = 1.25 or a 25.7% increase in sales from Week 1 to Week 2

Be sure to compare these sales increase numbers to your guest count numbers to see if your per person sales or average ticket amounts are increasing.

Formula: Weekly Sales/Number of Guests = Sales per Guest

Example: In the example above, there were 200 guests in week 1 and 220 in week 2. Therefore, the per guest sales increased as follows:

Week 1: 7000/200 = $35 per guest
Week 2: 8800/220 = $40 per guest.

Target Audience Growth

This refers to the growth in visits from a group that you designated, or have been concentrating on, is now growing. For example, before you start your efforts your store might have a mix of men, women, and kids shopping at the store. If your word of mouth and community efforts are directed to women, you would want to see that women are becoming a growing percentage of your overall customer base. This is a sign that your marketing and service efforts are succeeding. Again, this can be done with a simple tally at the cash register.

Formula: Number of Target Audience Customers/Total Number of Customers

Apply these measurements for subsequent weeks for tracking.
Example: Your target is women. During week 1, you have 200 customers. Of these, 85 are women. During week 2, you have 220 customers. Of these, 110 are women.

> Week 1: 85/200 = 43% of customers are in your target.
> Week 2: 110/220 = 50% of customers are in your target.
>   50 – 43 = 7% increase in women customers.

The next step is to measure the purchases of these target customers using this formula:

Formula: $\dfrac{\text{Purchases of Target Audience Customers}}{\text{Purchases of All Customers}}$ = % of Target Sales

Example: In week 1, your store sales are $50,000. In week 2, your store sales are $60,000. In week 1, women spent $25,000 in your store. In week 2, they spent $35,000.

> Week 1 target sales: 25,000/50,000 = 50% of sales made by women
> Week 2 target sales: 35,000/60,000 = 58% of sales made by women

CUSTOMER SERVICE MEASUREMENTS THAT INDICATE CHANGES IN YOUR BUSINESS

Now we move into a group of measurements that is less bottom line–oriented but is equally as important to your business. Many of these are ideas that you have already thought about or noticed in your store. Now is the time to formalize the measurement systems to be able to connect them to the changes you see in your business.

Employee Turnover

Why is this important? Because low employee turnover shows continuity. Guests feel it is important to see the same faces on a regular basis. It improves the overall relationship between your guests and the store. The fewer new employees, or the more consistent employees they see, the better they feel about the service they are going to receive. A good measurement of low turnover depends a little bit on the frequency of service you provide and the number of employees you have.

A benchmark you can use is roughly 100 percent turnover in a given year depending on your industry. High-turnover industries (such as restaurants) may have higher turnover rates. Clothing stores will have lower turnover rates. You measure that by looking at the number of W-2 forms your business has at the end of the year and compare it to the total number of employees working at your business at the end of the year. In a restaurant with 50 employees, 100 W-2 forms would indicate that you had 100 percent turnover. Your goal is to reduce your turnover, so if you had 100 percent turnover the first year, you might set a goal to have 75 percent turnover the next year and 50 percent turnover the year after that. If you have a clothing store with five employees, you might have a 28 percent turnover rate, and you might consider that to be an acceptable rate, or you might want to consider reducing it to 14 percent.

Guest Wait Time or Number of Walkouts

Another way to look at this is the number of walkouts you have in your store. You need to be watchful on how long your guests are waiting, even if they are not leaving your store. Even loyal guests who have to wait on a frequent basis may eventually go somewhere else.

You can measure this in a few ways. You can ask your salespeople or service staff to estimate the wait time they encounter on a daily basis. Asking them at the start of their shifts to notice this will help them to keep this in the back of their minds during the busy times of the day. At the end of the shifts, ask the staff to make a note on a chart as to whether they thought the wait times were average, fast, or slow. Also ask the salespeople to indicate if anything happened out of the ordinary that might have affected the wait times. For example, was there a large party at a restaurant, or was there a customer purchasing a lot of breakable items that took a long time to wrap up and package? You can also ask guests as they are leaving if they thought the wait time was acceptable.

Complaints as a Percentage of Overall Guest Visits

Record the number of complaints each week and compare it to total guest visits. A declining percentage is an indication of improving guest service. Ask your employees to keep a record of all complaints, and monitor whether the frequency of complaints change over time.

Formula: Total Complaints/Total Guests = Complaint Rate

Example: During week 1, you receive 15 complaints and have a total of 200 guests. During week 2, you receive 15 complaints and have a total of 220 guests.

At first glance, you may say "my complaints have not changed. . . . I have fifteen during one week and fifteen during the next week." However, if you use the formula you will see that your complaints per guest has decreased. This is one measurement that you will want to see decrease.

Week 1: 15 complaints/200 guests = 7.5% complaint rate
Week 2: 15 complaints/220 guests = 6.8% complaint rate

IN-STORE MEASUREMENTS

Another sign of the success of the program is that you can alter some of the ways you are doing business in order to increase your income. Here are some of the in-store signs to look for.

Ability to Increase Prices

Your ability to increase the price of your services in your store without losing guests is a sign of success. Ideally you should be able to gradually increase your prices as your guest count continues to grow. You should also look at cost of living measurements on an annual basis to see how your store is keeping up. This sign is an indicator that your guests value your service in increasing ways and are willing to pay a slightly higher price.

Declining Advertising Spending as a Percentage of Overall Sales Volume

Most of the programs we discuss in this book work side by side with traditional advertising programs. You should be able to reduce your traditional programs as you implement your word-of-mouth and community efforts. We do not expect that you will stop your regular advertising campaigns, but it is important to monitor changes relative to this advertising plan. For example, a good measurement is to analyze the amount you spend on advertising for several months relative to your total sales. If your sales are increasing while your ad spending remains constant, your percentage of advertising expense is actually decreasing. This means that your new guests added dollar volume, primarily from your word-of-mouth programs.

Formula: Advertising Spending per Month/Sales per Month = % Ad Spending

Example: During month 1 and month 2, you spend $10,000 on advertising per month. Sales increase from $65,000 to $85,000 from month 1 to month 2. (Remember, this is a measurement in which you want to see a decrease.)

Month 1: 10,000/65,000 = 15% ad spending
Month 2: 10,000/85,000 = 12% ad spending

WAYS TO MEASURE WORD-OF-MOUTH ACTIVITY

The science of measuring the impact and effects of word of mouth is still in its infancy. In the next several years, it is likely that we will see a lot more information about how to measure word of mouth. One of the benefits of using the Internet, though, is that techniques are now in place that allow you to track how people are using the information that you send out to them to start word-of-mouth campaigns.

Track Inquiries

Are people contacting you and asking you questions? What in particular are they questioning you about? You can use this information to measure the general level of interest in your store, and you can also think about additions or changes to your online information offerings based on what you read that people want to see.

Inquiries will occur in two places: online and in-store. The online inquiries are easy to track—simply count how many emails you get every day. You can even segment this count into some general categories (such as "questions about products and services," "questions about store hours and location," "questions about jobs") so you can track the general type of things people are interested in.

What is important for this is not just the number but also the nature of the inquiries. Act on the inquiries—answer questions and respond to suggestions. The in-store inquiries are likely to happen on a more informal basis, and you should get your employees involved in noting and tracking such questions. Again, this can be done with a simple tally at the register. Also, be sure you encourage your employees to use such questions as a way to develop conversations with the people who are asking the questions, and using those conversations to learn more about what customers really want (refer to Chapter 3 if you need a refresher course in this area!).

Receipt and Usage of Email

Start your tracking with measuring how many emails you send, how many you receive, and how many regular emailers are part of the community. In addition, services such as Constant Contact and Talisma (contact information at www.underdognetwork.com) allow you to track whether people who receive your email open the messages. These programs can also let you know whether someone forwards the email to family and friends. This is a great passive measurement that can help you know which types of emails are of most interest to your customers.

For every email that you sent, then, you will want to look at proportions.

Formula: Emails Opened/Emails Sent = Read Rate

Example: Let us say the first email or newsletter you sent out 500 emails to customers. The computer program indicates that 375 of these were opened and read.

375/500 = 75% read rate.

You will use this as a benchmark to measure future emails and newsletters. In a perfect world, the read rate will increase with each mailing. If it decreases, review the mailing to see if you did something different that might affect the read rate. Correct it for the next mailing and see if the read rate improves.

You will also want to track the pass-along of the emails; this is a measure of word of mouth. Computer programs can track the pass-along.

Formula: Emails Forwarded to Others/Emails Sent = Pass-Along Rate

Example: Of that first mailing of 500 emails, 60 were forwarded from one recipient to a new recipient:

60/500 = 12% pass-along rate.

This 12 percent would be your benchmark, and you should check each subsequent mailing to see if pass-along increases or decreases. If it decreases, it means that the contents were not of great interest to the readers. Evaluate and refine your contents for your next email.

Track Downloads of the Information That You Post

Here's another great technique that a computer program can track for you automatically. Track the frequency of downloads of any type of information you post at your Web site. Also, track the number of visitors to your most popular pages on your Web site. This will give you a great idea of what types of things people are (and are not) interested in as well as being able to compare the popularity of certain types of information. Use this to plan out future information you will give out.

Online programs can measure the number of hits (total visit occasions to your site, meaning multiple visits by an individual are counted) and unique visitors (total individuals visiting your site, meaning multiple visits by an individual are not counted).

Formula: $\dfrac{\text{Total Downloads}}{\text{Unique Visitors}}$ = Download Rate (% of visitors downloading)

Example: Let us say your site gets 800 unique visitors. A single piece of information (for example, an online flier on holiday gifts) is downloaded sixty-four times.

64/800 = 8% download rate for that flier

Track the topics of the information that you have available to download, and the download rate, and you will be able to have a record of the types of information that are of interest to your visitors and those that are not.

Track Registrations for Future Mailings

Email should provide an opt-out feature that allows people to automatically stop receiving your messages. Use this information to track your retention rate for your email program every other month.

Formula: $\dfrac{\text{\# of People Not Opting Out}}{\text{\# of People Receiving Emails}}$ = Retention Rate

Example: You have 500 people on your email list, and 100 people "opt out" of receiving them. Thus, 400 people reconfirm by not opting out that they wish to continue receiving your emails.

400/500 = 80% retention rate

By watching opt-out rates, you can track the number of people who do and do not like to receive your emails. You can see how your retention is affected during the course of your program. You are also taking advantage of an interaction opportunity: Find out what your customers would like to see in the newsletters in order to make them even more relevant to customers.

Track Those Joining Your Referral and Loyalty Programs

You will want to track the number of people who are joining any reward and referral programs that you set up, as well as how they found out about the program. In addition to the actual number of people who are joining, you will want to track whether they heard about the program from other customers. This will give you some indication of how well your WOM program is working. This can easily be done when someone is filling out an information form to join your program. Have a question that reads something like, "how did you hear about our program?" and give several check boxes for people to indicate their choice (i.e., from an advertisement, from an employee in the store, from your Web site, from someone who shops here). Leave a blank for them to fill in the name of the person who told them about it, if that is their choice, and then follow up with a thank-you note to the person who gave the referral.

Sales from Persons Involved in WOM and Community Program

Using the formulas that you've learned in this chapter, you can begin to measure the impact of other specific groups of customers in your store and to see if their shopping habits are changing. For example, you could compare purchases of people who are involved in WOM to your store to those who do not participate in WOM.

Formula: $\dfrac{\text{Purchases of Customers Involved in WOM}}{\text{Purchases of All Customers}} = \dfrac{\%\ \text{of Sales from}}{\text{WOM Customers}}$

Example: In week 1, your store sales are $50,000. In week 2, your store sales are $60,000. In week 1, customers involved in WOM spent $15,000 in your store. In week 2, they purchased $25,000.

Week 1 target sales: 15,000/50,000 = 30% of sales made by target
Week 2 target sales: 25,000/60,000 = 42% of sales made by target

You could also compare purchases of people who are involved in reward or referral programs to your store to those who are not involved in these programs.

Formula: $\dfrac{\text{Purchases of Program Customers}}{\text{Purchases of All Customers}} = \dfrac{\%\ \text{of Sales Made by}}{\text{Program Customers}}$

Example: In week 1, your store sales are $50,000. In week 2, your store sales are $60,000. In week 1, program customers purchased $30,000 in your store. In week 2, they purchased $40,000.

Week 1 target sales: 30,000/50,000 = 60% of sales made by target customers
Week 2 target sales: 40,000/60,000 = 67% of sales made by target customers

Finally, you could compare purchases of people who are involved in your online community to your store to those who are not involved in these programs.

Formula: $\dfrac{\text{Purchases of Community Members}}{\text{Purchases of All Customers}} = \dfrac{\%\ \text{of Sales Made by}}{\text{Community Members}}$

Example: In week 1, your store sales are $50,000. In week 2, your store sales are $60,000. In week 1, community members purchased $12,000 in your store. In week 2, they purchased $20,000.

Week 1 target sales = 12,000/50,000 = 24% of sales made by target
Week 2 target sales = 20,000/60,000 = 33% of sales made by target

Depending on your point-of-sale tracking system, you may be able to track the purchase of those who are involved with one of your efforts, such as those loyal customers who are part of your WOM program, those who are part of a reward or referral program, and those who are part of your online community. You can compare their purchases to the purchases of people who are not participating in any of these programs. This may be as simple as entering a code during the transaction, or you can track via a card or membership number. This method relies on your salespeople remembering to ask about this, and for people being honest in their declarations. However, such a metric can provide a very compelling story as to what your efforts are doing to your bottom line.

MEASURING THE VALUE OF YOUR COMMUNITY

You will want to estimate how your online community is affecting how people perceive your business. The Toolbox contains a primer on how Web sites can provide some levels of visitor data. Once you have a mechanism in place to collect that data, here are a few of the ways that they can be used to assess the value of your community.

Track Those Joining the Online Community

Your online bulletin board program is likely to give you the ability to track who is joining and who is leaving the community, as well as how frequently they visit and post to the community (see the Toolbox for more information on how to set this up). This is done through having a private community where people have to register to belong (see Chapter 6).

You will want to keep track of the following on a monthly basis:

- Current members: people who have been members of the community for a full month as of the first of the month. Example: Everyone on February 1 who has been a member since January 1.
- New members: people who have joined since the first of the month. In the example given above, people who joined in January.
- Lapsed members: people who have not logged in during the past month (in the example above, during the month of January). Please note that lapsed members are *not* members who do not post; you will have members who have logged in who are not active participants in your community.

Formula: Total Members = Current + New Members – Lapsed Members

You will want your total members to increase over time. Here's how to track this:

Formula: Total Members Month 2 / Total Members Month 1 = New Member Growth

Example: On March 1, you have 100 current members, 20 new members, and 10 lapsed members. On April 1, you have 115 current members, 25 new members, and 12 lapsed members.

Total Members March 1: 100 + 20 − 10 = 110 Total Members
Total Members April 1: 115 + 25 −12 = 128 Total Members
128/110 = 1.16 or 16% growth rate

Number of Visits and Comments

Your activity log will be able to give you the total number of "log ins" and the total number of different members logging in to your site during a specified period (say a month). Use this to track your total visits, as well as your visits per person.

Formula: Total Visits/Total Members Logging In = Visits per Person

Example: Recall from the previous example that you have 110 members in March and 128 members in April. Your total visits went from 800 in March to 1000 in April.

Visits per person for March = 800/110 = 7.27 per person, or the average person logged on about once every four or five days
Visits per person for April = 1000/128 = 7.82 per person, or the average person logged on about twice per week

Time Spent with Community Content

The number of consumers' posts and the amount of time spent on your site shows that you have moved a consumer to become committed to the community. Your activity log should be able to give you an average time per visit count. Track these over a monthly basis to see if the time spent with your community is increasing.

Formula: Time Spent Month 2/Time Spent Month 1 = Change in Time Spent

Example: During March, each visit lasted 4 minutes 15 seconds (or 255 seconds). During April, each visit lasted 5 minutes 36 seconds (336 seconds).

336/255 = 1.31 or 31% increase in average time spent per visit

Tone of the Community

Finally, all the formulas in the world will not give you the most important information that you want to know: how people feel about your store. Try to read as many of the posts at the community as possible. Listen to the tone of the postings at your community. Do you hear positive things about your company? Negative things? Does the tone of the comments change over time?

TAKING IT FURTHER: MAKING SENSE OF MEASURES

There's many formulae here, a lot of math . . . and we do not expect you to implement all these for your own store. What else can you do with all this information? We encourage you to look beyond sales to have a better understanding of what is going well at your store. It is the way to measure the strength of your community and the success of all your efforts. Moreover, it gives you more that you can talk about with your customers and your staff.

Though there may be certain information that you do not feel comfortable telling everyone (such as the exact dollar amount of your sales), consider sharing some of your success stories with your customers and your staff. For instance, the percentage increase in sales and the increase in number of community members might be good numbers to share. Also, do not be afraid to address some of the measurements that may not be so good. For example, if your complaints are increasing, having a real number to talk about with your employees may make the issue a bit more tangible than a comment such as "we seem to be getting more complaints lately." Using numbers to set goals is also something that works well with many employees.

SUMMING UP

In this chapter, we have shown you:

- Why measurement is important.
- Different customers and sales measurements that can track your success.
- That customer service measurements can add depth to the sales numbers.
- Ways to track the impact of word of mouth and community programs.
- How to use information to motivate employees.

Clearly, there are many ways you can track, monitor, and measure what's happening with your business. The bottom line is that these measurements are tools for you to assess your activities and their affects. We have more tools for you in the next chapter to find ways to keep your community fresh.

Chapter **9**

Keeping Your Community Fresh and Vital

Customers → Conversations → Community → *Commitment*

We have gone over most of the tools you need to get started on your word-of-mouth efforts. At this point, we hope you will take some time and map out a first-year plan for your activities. In this chapter, we include techniques for keeping your efforts fresh. These are things to keep in mind through the year as you build your word-of-mouth program and promote your community presence.

The most important thing to remember is that you just cannot start the program and let it run on its own. Throughout this book we have encouraged you to maintain a presence in your activities. Word of mouth and community building are not things you try once. They differ from your traditional advertising in that they need consistent tending and nurturing. Think of them as bonfires that you build to light the way to your store. Don't let the fire go out!

In the Getting Started section, we tell you about cluster effects and the value of patience in letting your community develop. In the Moving Forward section, we talk about some of the things you need to keep in mind to keep your communication efforts vibrant and engaging for your customers. We provide a list of action steps for you to consider. In the Taking It Further section, we discuss efforts and technologies that can enhance your community.

Read this chapter while you are getting some of your programs started, and then refer back to it in a month or two once they become established. These are all actions that will enhance your community. You can think about doing some of these down the road or perhaps even scheduling them into your annual plan. The most important thing to remember, though, is that your community is a dynamic organism: It is constantly changing, and part of your job is to be involved in keeping those changes relevant and meaningful to the community members.

GETTING STARTED: THE CLUSTER EFFECT AND ITS IMPACT ON YOUR COMMUNITY

First, let us consider a few things you can do to surprise your customers, fit into the lives of the members of your community, and allow your community members to make the site their own. We end with some notes on what your role in the community should be.

Allow for the Cluster Effect to Take Hold

We live in a fast-paced world. We want to put things into practice and see the results immediately. Remember, though, that both word of mouth and community building are not things that happen over night. They are not ads that run in the newspaper Friday morning and bring in traffic throughout the weekend. These types of messages require trust and interest from the people receiving the messages, and this may take a little bit of time. The cluster effect is your friend in this regard.

The *cluster effect* is an economic theory of forecasting that basically says that buyers and sellers of a particular good or service congregate in a certain place and hence induce other buyers and sellers to relocate there as well. Because of the cluster effect, certain industries are located in certain cities, such as the U.S. automotive industry in Detroit and the high fashion industry in Paris. While there may be slight economic advantages for businesses to locate in the specific geographic area, the reason that the cluster effect takes hold is simply because that geographic area becomes, psychologically, the place to be for buyers and sellers that wish to part of the industry. Proximity can facilitate knowledge networks and interactive relationships between the buyers and sellers in the cluster.[1]

For online communities, the cluster effect occurs when buyers and sellers (in this case, of information) begin to congregate in a specific geographic area (in this case, the online community). As more individuals congregate at the online community, they spread the word about the community to others that they know with similar interests. Thus, the online community becomes the place to be for individuals with a specific interest. This will not happen overnight, as it takes time for the information about your community to work its way through the Store Champions, the Family, and possibly to the Flirts and the Phantoms. As the creator of the community and the originator of all the initial messages about the community, you need to be able to convince your best customers to participate in word of mouth or try the online community. Once they try it, you need to get them to be enthusiastic about it and encourage their friends and family to be part of the community. Thus, one person encourages a small group, a cluster, to become part of the community.[2]

A current example of how the cluster effect works can be seen in the popular social networking site MySpace, one of the most popular online communities for teens and college students. When did you start to hear about MySpace? It was probably sometime during 2006. You might be surprised, then, to learn that MySpace was actually started several years before that, in 2004, by several entrepreneurs whose previous dot-com efforts had failed. Today, MySpace and competing social networking sites are everywhere. A recent study by the Pew Center on Internet Life found that 70 percent of teen girls and 57 percent of teen boys have profiles on these networking sites, the top ones being MySpace and Facebook.[3]

For the first three years of its existence, MySpace had a very slow growth rate. You may be surprised about this, since in 2007 MySpace is everywhere in the news. However, MySpace received no publicity or media coverage for the first two years of its existence. Its growth was completely organic, which allowed for cluster effects, which are highly important for any type of word-of-mouth or community experience.

Once you get a core group of people to participate in your community, they will get others interested as long as the dialogue within the group is interesting. Selecting the correct social glue is the way to make this happen. Then you can tell others not in the core group about the success of the effort in order to convince them to follow along. Then this second group becomes, in essence, part of the core group, and the cluster effects continue. Remember we talked about the types of rewards in earlier chapters. Well, this is another reason why rewards and recognition are so important—to reinforce the value of the community so the individuals can pass on the value to the others in their social circles.

But back to our original point: Since there's so much communication and decision making taking place, you need to give the program time to develop and take hold. That is why thinking about your plan on annual basis is important.

Once you get some basic activities going, make a point of checking out a new Internet resource once a week to keep on top of news and information. Go to a search engine (such as Google) and put in a search term such as "hair salon new products" or "restaurant menu ideas" and see what you come up with.

Use this information to plan a monthly information event that people will start to expect and anticipate. For example, have a monthly update of new products that are arriving at your store that month or a list of new menu items or services that will be available in the upcoming month. You can even think about a try-it price that you might offer on one of the new items. These special events will also help the cluster effect take hold.

Ask people for feedback on the information you are sharing with them. Always remember to ask the people who receive your communications to forward them along to their friends. Also, ask them for feedback on the information that you provide. Do they like it, do they find it helpful? Ask them what they want to learn about. This will give you more ideas on what to pursue for your own communications.

Action Idea: Make sure the cluster effect will happen by continuing to give your customers interesting and relevant information to use and to respond to. Use your sales contacts, and ask people in your business what email lists they subscribe to and what Web sites they visit. These can be great sources for news and information. For example, the About.com Web site issues a weekly newsletter with a compilation of retail news. Find out more about it at retail industry.about.com/library/blnewsletter.htm. Other online information regarding specific businesses are listed below. More are listed at our Web site, www.underdognetwork.com. Use these sources to regularly update your content and create conversations with your community.

Fashion	www.dnrnews.com
	www.footwearnews.com
	www.wwd.com
Electronics and appliances	www.smartbrief.com/news/cea
	www.twice.com
	news.com.com
Restaurants	www.restaurantnews.com
	www.nrn.com
Salons	www.interhair.com
Auto repair and parts	www.aftermarket.org/Home.asp
Pet stores	www.petville.com
Home improvement stores	www.homechannelnews.com

MOVING FORWARD: UNDERSTANDING THE POWER OF SOCIAL NETWORKS THROUGH MYSPACE

We cannot state enough how important it is to listen to your customers and respond to them. Thank them for their communications, and take what they tell you to heart. Find ways to improve your community based on what your customers are telling you. Make the community exactly what your visitors want it to be. Social technologies succeed when they fit into the social lives and practices of those who engage with the technology. For example, MySpace did not try to force people's usage habits into its ideas of what it should be.[4] Instead, the originators of MySpace let users' activities evolve as they saw fit. As the site evolved, it moved from simply being profiles of individuals to a way for people to connect with others, to advertise bands and social activities, and to comment on the greater world around them. Today, MySpace is the largest social networking site with hundreds of thousands of visitors every day.

We are not expecting you to be another MySpace. However, you can take some of the lessons from its success and apply it to your own efforts. Young people flocked to MySpace at a time when no other site allowed them to create a personalized space all their own. They wanted to take advantage of everything the Internet had to offer and to express themselves, and MySpace did not hold them back. And that is the key lesson for you to consider. It provided a nurturing environment for people wanting to accomplish certain goals, and it grew by virtue of that fact.

We have talked about the importance of social glue, and the lesson from MySpace is that once you have determined what your social glue is, you need to let the interest and excitement develop on its own. You can nurture it, of course, by continually reinforcing the importance of the social glue and providing new information or opportunities for interactions.

Be wary of placing any types of limits on your activities surrounding the social glue. Limiting what can be done or said relative to the social glue in your efforts can be the kiss of death. However, allowing the social glue to be developed, strengthened, and broadened on its own will lead to success. In fact, it can result in your efforts becoming something referred to as cultural currency.

The currency we are most familiar with, of course, is money—cold hard cash. Cultural currency is similar in that it is something that is shared, exchanged, and valued. It is highly likely that your social glue will involve the sharing and exchanging of information about a particular topic. When this information becomes valued, when the information people are finding from you and your efforts is important, unique, and necessary to them, then the information becomes cultural currency. Being "in the know" is more powerful than money.

Efforts that involve cultural currency become highly popular. What becomes cultural currency depends, of course, on the group of people in your community. For the generation now in its teens and twenties, music is cultural currency. Many young people are interested in and closely follow music and celebrities. Other young people follow the young people that follow music. They want to know what their peers think is cool and fresh. Music played a critical role in increasing the popularity of social networking sites like MySpace, simply by giving it cultural currency among celebrities and by marking the site as "cool." (Even teens that do not care about music recognize that music differentiates people and is part of the cool narrative.)

Similarly, MySpace has created the concept of friends as a way of having cultural currency. Part of the value of a community is creating a social network. Your online community will become a network naturally as people register to be part of the community. MySpace has taken this to the next level by encouraging people to create their own network of online friends. For some people, having a large network of friends is currency and assists in their self-identification. We are not suggesting, of course, that you copy MySpace. But you should keep an eye out for the things that your customers are interested in, that they value and share. That could become your cultural currency, something you will want to talk about and use to keep your community fresh.

How do you put these lessons from MySpace into practice?

- Think about your social glue in every decision you make, every message you send out.
- Keep an eye out for anything related to your social glue. Think about doing a Google news search once a month to find out what is in the news about the topic. Find interesting sites that cover music, parenting, gardening, car racing. Find new and interesting links that you can share with your community.
- Get your employees involved in also keeping you up to date on the newest Web sites that address your social glue. Credit them in your messages with finding the best sites. Perhaps even ask them to write reviews of the sites they find.
- Ask others in your audience to share what they find, too. Ask people to email news or information to you, and then you can email out to the rest of the audience. Be sure to thank (and credit) the people who send you the information. This will get people comfortable in sending you information and they will look for their names in future messages.

This last step is a great way to encourage users to make the site their own. Even though you will be adding information to your online community and providing information to your customers via email, you will want to use their input to modify the site. For example, with the poll idea, ask them to suggest a poll that you can implement in the future. For your online community, you will want to let your users define the culture. The Internet allows people to create and develop their own identities. It allows users to take ownership of the presentation of self and personalize it to present the face they want to present to the online world.

Successful sites like MySpace evolved with its users, building a trusting relationship, figuring out how to meet their needs and cultural desires, providing them with features and really trying to give them what they were looking for. Identity development requires taking ownership of your presentation of self and really being able to create who you are in your online environment.

KEEPING INTEREST AND INVOLVEMENT ALIVE

People often say that social networking sites will succeed when people have something to *do*. They point to sites like LinkedIn.com where businesspeople can network socially and actually get "value" out of the site. That works for LinkedIn because their social glue is making business connections, and their cultural capital is business connections. However, formalized actions and tangible benefits, such as those at LinkedIn, are not the only path to success. However, the reality is that most people's social lives are not so formal, not so action-oriented. At this point, you might be saying, "Don't I have to make sure there's always something new, something do to at my community site?" Not really. Do not worry too much about giving people something to do or having a completely formalized presence and agenda. You will want to participate, but you will not want to be the only one setting the agenda and framing the discussion. Once again, it all goes back to your social glue.

Even when there's no prescribed activity, people will be doing things on your sites. They are hanging out, they are exploring, they are learning, and perhaps most important, they are meeting new people. They are thinking about things they have purchased and will purchase in the future. They are building relationships through sharing. They are being entertaining and being entertained. They are spending an important cultural capital: their time.

Action Idea: Use polls to learn what's on the community's mind and to keep things fresh. Once every few weeks, post a question of the people in your community. This can be different from a poll in that you will provide an open-ended forum at your online community that allows people more room to explain their answers. This will stimulate discussion, which is the best way for your community to feel ownership. Some example questions are posted here.

If you're a	Consider this type of question to spur discussion
Restaurant	What do you like best about going out to eat? What irks you the most?
Apparel store	What do you think of the new spring fashion trends? What do you think you will be buying and what do you think you will be skipping?
Pet store	Do you own an exotic pet? Which one? If you could own any animal as a pet, what would you own and why?
Bookstore	What was your favorite book when you were a child? Why?
Craft store	What craft would you like to learn this year? Why?
Automotive repair store	What tips do you have for winterizing your car?

When you are thinking of ways to take things further, one thing that you may think about is to add some technological innovations to your community. This is a great idea! It also may worry you a bit, especially if you are not the most technically astute person on the planet. In fact, you may think that people want things that are easy to navigate and learn how to use. While that is true for some of your customers, many people do not want or need simplicity. Some online community sites have failed when they focus on being simple and narrow, and they have given users very limited options as to what they can do. Don't be afraid to have a few bells and whistles at your site.

What types of innovations should you think about? Streaming video and audio are two possibilities. The popularity of YouTube suggests that people love to create videos and watch the videos produced by others. You might consider including promotional videos for new products or services, highlight videos of an event held at your store, or interviews with experts on specific topics. Similarly, people enjoy downloading podcasts to their iPods or their computers to hear new information. You also might want to consider adding a search feature, so people can find past conversations that they have enjoyed or be able to find archived information about a topic in which they are interested. Or think about providing an online poll that will stimulate discussion about something connected with your store. What about a "what new dessert should we add?" poll for a restaurant?

Action Idea: Introduce a new technology or online offering once a month. Try something new like a poll or a game and monitor how people react to it. Online polls, for example, are fun and quick ways for your customers to interact with your Web site and with you. People will answer the poll and then check to see how their answer compared to others. They may also send the poll along to their friends. There are several free sources for online poll software:

- www.easy-poll.com
- www.surveypopups.com
- www.thefreecountry.com/scripthosting/polls.shtml

Here are some example poll questions that you could use on your site.

If you're a . . .	*Try this poll . . .*
Restaurant	What do you have for dessert most often? A: Ice cream; B: Cookies; C: Pie; D: Other
Hair salon	How often do you get a haircut? A: Monthly; B: Every two months; C: Whenever it is too long
Pet store	Do you buy your pets holiday and birthday presents? A: Of course! They are at the top of the list; B: Occasionally, if I remember; C: No, I do not
Apparel store	Do you read fashion magazines? A: The minute they hit the newsstand! B: I subscribe to a few; C: If I have some spare time I might; D: No, I do not
Electronics store	Which high-definition platform are you considering? A: HD-DVD; B: Blu ray; C: Other

Garden store	What types of tomatoes will you plant this year? A: Beefsteak; B: Cherry; C: Paste; D: Standard; E: I am not planting tomatoes this year
Computer store	What type of Internet access do you have at home? A: Dial-up; B: Cable modem; C: DSL; D: Other; E: I do not have Internet access at home
Automotive repair store	How often do you change your oil? A: Every 3000 miles; B: Every 4000 miles; C: Every 5000 miles

Whatever you add to your site, if it works and people like it, leave it up. If they do not like it, take it down. Ask for feedback on the addition to make the decision.

There are many other sources online for tools to add to your site and to your community. You can also contact your ISP and see if they have any special tools or items you can add to your page. Check online at these types of offerings:

- mediabuilder.com
- www.thefreesite.com
- www.free-counters.co.uk

You may be concerned that something will happen with the technology and you will get a glitch or a bug in the system that may affect what people can do on your site. If you do get some type of technological glitch, all we can tell you is not worry about it too much. Get it fixed and get the community back up as soon as you can. Bugs and glitches make technologies seem alive, particularly once you have acknowledged that they occurred and you fix them. Do not be worried that a glitch in your email or at your community site will make people run screaming from the message, never to return. Bugs in your system will signal to your customers that you are a real person, not an automaton. When the bug is fixed, you can send out a message apologizing for the bug and explaining what happened—another chance for an interaction. If the new technology does not work for your community—if it crashes your system constantly or if people just hate it—then take it down and apologize. You are human, you will make mistakes. It is all part of life in your community.

TAKING IT FURTHER: REVISITING YOUR MARKETING GRID

We have talked a lot about your marketing grid in this book, and we hope you have been keeping it updated with your plans and ideas. There's a lot to be said for having an annual communications plan: It organizes your time, it allows your customers to have a good idea of when to expect communications from you, and of course it allows you to track your progress. You will also have a handle on your budget and how much you are spending on these efforts.

That said, you should plan little surprises for your customers. What do we mean by *surprises*? These are short-term, quick events that allow you to try new things and give your customers little treats and perks. They can also address some of your short-term business issues.

Let's say you have a service business like a restaurant or salon and find that at certain times, say Wednesdays from 2 to 4 p.m., your place of business is empty. Why not send out a quick email on Monday and say "On Wednesday from 2 to 4, come in for a 50 percent off dessert" or "Call now to make an appointment for a special deal on highlights on Wednesday afternoons." This is a fun way to surprise and treat your customers and to get them to sample something that they might not try without the surprise.

> **Action Idea:** Think about offering a surprise once a month or so. Analyze your business, and schedule your surprise during low sales periods. Keep track of the people who participate in your surprise, and encourage them to pass on the surprise to someone else they know.

Some example surprises are outlined here.

If you're a . . .	*The surprise could be . . .*
Apparel or accessories store	A discount on sandals or belts on a certain day at a certain time.
Automotive store	Offer $20 oil changes during times of the week where you do not have many other repairs scheduled.
Camera store	Offer discount developing during those times of day when you are not busy.

TAKING IT FURTHER: CLARIFYING COMMUNITY ROLES

The people who participate in your efforts will, of course, recognize that there is an individual, one single person, who is the master behind the architecture of the effort. There's someone who controls access and, conceivably, controls the interactions on the sites. In order to be successful, your customers must trust that the creators of the community (and that would be you) have their best interests in mind. If you let your community develop on its own, then your customers are investing a lot of time and energy into creating their own identity as part of the effort. And they will want to be confident that the time they spend at your community is worth it

Having too heavy a hand in how the system is run will destroy the trust that your customers have in you as the leader of your community. Of course, there are good reasons to have a heavy hand at time: You will want to keep out spammers and kick off malicious users or trolls. Nevertheless, begin with the idea that everyone is a valued member of your community and assume that individuals are participating openly and respectfully, only step in when necessary to keep harmony in your community.

At the same time, be careful of how your commercial messages interact with the social glue. You do not want your community to feel that you are sending "buy this now" messages down their throats. To accomplish this, just be aware that not every message you post should be a commercial. Participate in the community as an interested person who is involved in the social glue, and let the commercial messages come naturally.

You should personally welcome as many new users to your online community as you can, perhaps with an email that encourages them to read the conversations and discussions to discover the content and tone of the forum. Use biographies of moderators or guest experts to make new people feel more familiar with the forum. You should also encourage them to post when they feel comfortable with the community. If possible, recognize frequency of people's participation. Perhaps give out stars every 100 posts, or recognize the most interesting posts or questions in a separate discussion at the community. This recognizes the importance of every individual in contributing to the discussion and the community.

Recognize the quality of your members' participation. In addition to frequency of participation, which we discussed in the previous section, also think about recognizing the quality of participation and recognizing those participants whose posts are informative, interesting, or humorous. There may be some other type of post you wish to recognize. We encourage you to do so.

This recognition can take many forms. For example, you can use voting/ moderation to let the community pick its favorite post of the month. You could utilize some sort of brownie points system in which members earn credits for good contributions, which are displayed by their name. The easiest method, though, might be to move posts that people like and attract a lot of discussion into a "best of" section at your community Web site. This is a great place to highlight interesting posts, and it also gives new members a specific place to start learning about your community. Finally, think about writing a regular column or posting area to write about things that are happening to you and your store relative to the social glue.

SUMMING UP

In this chapter we have showed you:

- What the cluster effect is and what it means for your community.
- Tips on where you can find information to keep your community fresh.
- The importance of cultural currency.

- How to surprise customers.
- Ways to integrate innovative technologies into your community.

Building an inviting place that attracts users and maintaining high-quality content on a bustling community site is far from easy, but these key points should help get you going in the right direction. One last thing for you to consider is your role as an ethical communicator in today's marketplace. That is what we discuss in the next chapter.

Chapter **10**

Ethical Considerations That Will Make Your Community More Successful

Customers → Conversations → Community → *Commitment*

In this chapter, we discuss two of the key ethical issues that confront any business that collects information and uses that information to send messages to customers and potential customers: privacy and transparency. *Privacy*, specifically information privacy, refers to the ability of an individual or group to stop information about themselves from becoming known to people other than those they choose to give the information to. *Transparency* also refers to the ability of a receiver of information to recognize the source of the information. In part, your customers will decide the degree to which they trust you by virtue of how you approach privacy and transparency in your communications with them.

We discuss privacy and transparency separately and indicate some of the decisions that you should make regarding both. Additionally, we provide you with ideas on how you communicate your privacy and transparency policies to your customers.

WHY PRIVACY STATEMENTS ARE IMPORTANT

Consumers are concerned about privacy of their personal information. We hear about consumer issues with privacy most often when people are buying things online. They do not want their financial information, such as their credit card numbers, to be compromised. Consumers are concerned about identity theft, which can occur if someone can get access to a consumer's Social Security number and birth date.

It is likely that you will not need to collect any of these sensitive data from your customers, especially if you do not sell products or services online. Therefore, you may wonder why you need to be concerned about privacy. You should be concerned primarily because many consumers are worried simply with the amount of unsolicited email that they get every day. They think, and rightly so, that the more things that they sign up for using either their email or postal mail address, the more likely they are to get this unwanted information. And just for that reason, they may choose not to participate in your programs.

We recommend that you think about how you will use customer information, and how you will communicate that information to them. Having a firm privacy policy does many things. It helps build your credibility. It strengthens that bond of trust that is so important between you and your customers. Privacy policies can influence overall customer satisfaction. For example, a study by Forrester Research found that consumers who rate Web sites as doing a good job with the protection of personal information also have a high level of overall satisfaction with those Web sites. In addition, almost half of all consumers regularly look for privacy and security policies online. Finally, Forrester Research found that consumers will be more likely to purchase from companies that they find trustworthy.

When thinking about how you will approach customer information practices, we recommend that you start by following the Fair Information Practices (FIPs) established by the Federal Trade Commission (FTC). Complete information about the FIPs is available at www.ftc.gov/reports/privacy3/fairinfo.htm, and we have summarized the important information about the FIPs that you need to know in this chapter. These practices were designed to address key consumer issues and concerns about privacy of their personal information. Remember, you will be collecting some degree of personal information about your customers both online and offline during your information-gathering phases. People differ greatly in terms of their sensitivity to personal information. Some people are happy to tell you lots about themselves and do not care how safe that information is, while other people are more wary about much of their personal information. It is always best to err on the conservative side and make sure that all your customers feel safe when they share information with you. Remember, it is your customers' choice whether they give information to you or not. Making that choice one that your customers are happy with, though, is your responsibility, and following the FIPs is an excellent way to address any customer concerns.

It is easiest for your customers if you put the information together in a written privacy policy that you have on your Web site or that you can print up and distribute to your customers when they sign up for your messages. To be effective, such a disclosure should be clear and conspicuous, posted in a prominent location, and readily accessible from both the site's home page and any Web page where information is collected from the consumer. It should also be unavoidable and understandable so that it gives consumers meaningful and effective notice of what will happen to the personal information they are asked to divulge. In the next few pages, we will give you ways to craft your own privacy policy for your Web site and your community.

It is important to interject here that there are very strict U.S. laws on collecting information from children under the age of thirteen. We have assumed throughout this book that you are dealing mainly with people aged eighteen and over. Depending on your store, though, you may have customers under age eighteen. If you actively solicit information from children under the age of thirteen, you must familiarize yourself with the Children's Online Privacy Protection Act. Find it online at www.ftc.gov/bcp/conline/pubs/buspubs/coppa.htm.

While we provide information on the areas that you should address, we also encourage you to check out different Web sites that you visit and see how different companies handle their privacy policies. One thing that you will see is that often a company will announce in bold letters "we will never sell your personal information." For many customers, this is the biggest issue that they have regarding information collection. While selling of mailing lists can be very profitable, the fact that companies sell information often results in people refusing to give information. To start with, we recommend that you keep the personal information that you collect for your business only. In the future, if you want to share or trade information with another retailer or any other type of company, you can contact your customers and ask if they are okay with that. In the meantime, though, do not release your customer's or community's personal information to anyone; have complete control of their information at all times.

STEPS IN DEVELOPING AND IMPLEMENTING YOUR PRIVACY PROGRAM

There are five areas to consider when you put together your policy: notice, choice, access, integrity, and enforcement. We discuss each of them below and provide some possible language to use in your privacy policy after each area.

Notice/Awareness

The FTC notes that the most fundamental of the five principles is *notice*. If you do nothing else in your privacy policy, you should alert customers that you are collecting information about them before you actually start collecting that information. Moreover, three of the other principles discussed below—choice/consent, access/participation, and enforcement/redress—are only meaningful when a consumer has notice of your policy regarding notice.

Specifically, you should consider providing the following information to your customers before you collect any data:

- A specific statement that you are collecting the personal information about an individual.
- A list of the specific information you will be collecting (i.e., name, address, email address, purchase habits). You might also think about telling the customers what you will not be collecting: that specifically might be credit

card data, which many customers will be wary about providing to you if there are not strong safeguards for protection.

- A statement as to how you will use the data (e.g., to make sure customers are getting the information they need about the store, to keep users up to date about the store, to make changes in the store).
- An indication of who has access to the data (like people who work at your store).
- How you will collect the data (e.g., that you will use information given to you voluntarily by the customer, and if you will use data that you collect electronically from the customer).
- How you will ensure the confidentiality of the data; specifically, where the data will be stored and how access to the data is protected.

Writing the Policy

Here is some specific language you can use.

- When collecting email and postal mail addresses: "We will use your name and email/postal mail address to send you newsletters and other information about our store on a regular basis. We will never sell this information to a third party without your express permission. If you wish to be removed from our mailing list, just let us know."
- For other information that you collect via your Web site: "We collect personal information online, including names, postal and email addresses, and product preference and complaint information. We do not knowingly collect or maintain any personal information from children under the age of thirteen. In addition, no part of our sites are designed with the purpose of attracting any person under age thirteen. We will use your personal information only for the purpose for which it is submitted, such as to reply to your emails, handle your complaints, enroll you in programs, or place you on a list to receive further communication from us. We never sell or rent your personal information."

Choice/Consent

The second widely accepted core principle of FIP is consumer choice or consent. This means giving customers options as to how any personal information collected from them may be used once you have collected it. You have addressed this in the How You Will Use the Data section, and for most customers, the biggest concern is what is called secondary uses of information, that is, uses beyond the original purpose of the exchange.

When people sign up for your email list, tell them that by signing up they agree to receive electronic messages on a regular basis about your store. But the principle of choice relates not to this but to secondary uses of information—that is, uses beyond those necessary to complete the exchange (i.e., customers exchange information about *them* for information about *you*). Secondary uses of information would therefore be an external transfer, where you would give or sell the information to others. The principle of choice states that you would notify customers if you were planning such a transfer, and the customers would be able to agree or disagree to their information being part of the transfer.

Traditionally, two types of choice have been used: opt-in or opt-out. Opt-in is when your customers sign up at your store or Web site to receive the information you wish to provide to them. You can take this a step further by allowing your customers to indicate the types of information they would like to receive (information about sales, about new products, and so on). This increases the chances that your customers will not perceive your messages as unwanted spam. At the same time, ask your opting-in customers if it is all right if you provide their contact information to other companies with products and services that might be of interest to them. By doing this, you are making sure that you are protecting secondary usage of information.

It is always a good idea to remind your customers who have opted in that they previously indicated they were interested in receiving such email and that this is not spam. Additionally, give your customers the opportunity to be removed from the mailing list if they so choose.

The opt-out model is when you go ahead and send messages to a list of addresses that you've collected without the permission of the recipients of the messages. For example, you might have received the mailing list from a neighboring business who thought that its customers would be interested in your store. With opt-out, the message recipient would have to contact you directly to inform you he or she did not want to receive any additional messages.

Choice can also involve more than the yes/no options described above. Some marketers have allowed consumers to tailor the nature of the information they provide and the use of such information. For example, customers can be provided separate choices as to whether they wish to be on a mailing list about sales and promotions, a list about new products, a list about in-store events, a list about community marketing, or a marketing list sold to third parties. In order to be effective, any choice regime should provide a simple and easily accessible way for consumers to exercise their choices.

In the online environment, choice easily can be exercised by simply clicking a box on the computer screen that indicates a user's decision with respect to the use and/or dissemination of the information being collected.

Writing the Policy

Language you can use:

- For any type of mailing: "At any time, you can add or remove your name from our mailing list by contacting us at *<your email address>*."

- For mailings and for your online community: "We do not sell or rent your personal information. If we find an opportunity that may be of interest to you, we will contact you for your permission before we undertake this transaction."

Access/Participation

Access is the third core principle, and it refers to how you make the customer's information available to them for review. Additionally, it suggests that customers can revise any information that they feel is inaccurate or incomplete. The purpose of this principle is to make sure that the profile of the individual based on their information is as true to life as it can be.

You have a couple of choices regarding this principle. If you have all your data in an electronic file, you could set up a system to allow your customers to access their data and correct or delete any information that they wish. What might be easier for you, though, is to offer to provide any customer a print-out of their information file at a time that is convenient to both of you. The customer can review it and provide you with updates or corrections in writing.

Writing the Policy

Language you can use:

- For both email and your online community: "Email us if you wish to see the information we have collected about you for completeness and accuracy."

Integrity/Security

The fourth widely accepted principle is that data be accurate and secure. This was touched on briefly in the Notice section, in that you need to inform your customers how the information is kept safe. Data integrity is a bit more complex. To ensure data integrity, you should take reasonable steps to make sure that your data is correct—that information can be corrected by consumers if necessary, and that untimely data will be destroyed or converted to anonymous form. While we addressed allowing consumer access to the data in the previous section, you should take a moment to think about how long you should keep the data that you collect. While some customers may be part of your Family for a long time, others may come and go. You might want to set a policy that you will destroy any data from inactive members (such as people who opt out of your program or move away from your city) after a certain period of time—say, nine months to a year.

Security involves your measures to protect against any unauthorized access to the data that could lead to the information from your customers being used for purposes not intended by you and your customers. In most cases, you will store your data on a computer. Is there password access to the computer, and do only a few people know the password? In addition to these measures, which are referred to as managerial measures, there's also a level of technical security measures that you might investigate. Technical security measures to prevent unauthorized access include encryption in the transmission and storage of data and the storage of data on secure servers or computers that are inaccessible by modem, so that someone from the outside cannot hack into your system.

Writing the Policy

Suggested language:

- For emails and your online community: "We have taken steps to ensure that your personal information is secure. Data that is not used for communicating electronically is stored on a computer without Internet access. Store personnel with access to personal information obtained on our Web sites must adhere to all aspects of this privacy policy as part of their employment contract."
- For emails: "Email that you send us is not necessarily secure against interception. If your email communication includes sensitive information like your Social Security number, your bank account number, or your credit or charge card numbers, please do not contact us through email; instead, call us at *<phone number>*."

Enforcement/Redress

The final principle for the FIPs addresses enforcement and redress. Essentially, it discusses what types of mechanisms are in place to ensure the policies you have developed are followed (enforcement) and to allow means of recourse by parties who believe they were not treated fairly by your information collection practices (redress). If you allow your customers to review their information, opt out of practices they do not wish to participate in, and safeguard their information, you will not have to worry about redress.

Writing the Policy

Suggested language:

- For emails and your online community: "Customers who have questions, concerns, or complaints about our handling of their privacy and confidentiality rights should send us an email or a written letter detailing your concerns. We will respond in a timely manner and may conduct a privacy investigation or review of policy and procedures."

Another way to address enforcement is with independent companies that assess your policies and provide a seal verifying that they are appropriate.

These companies charge a fee for this analysis, but the seal is a strong signal to your visitors that they can trust your policies. BBB Online has a seal specifically for companies that do not engage in financial transactions online. Additionally, several of the sites (PrivacyBot and Guardian eCommerce) will write your privacy policies for you. If you are not collecting financial information, you probably do not need a seal, but if you plan someday to dip your toe in the online commerce waters, a seal may be necessary. Some of the best-known companies involved with seal programs include:

- TrustE: www.truste.org
- BBB Online: www.bbbonline.org
- Guardian eCommerce: www.guardianecommerce.net
- PrivacyBot: www.privacybot.com
- Privacy Secure: www.privacysecure.com

TRANSPARENCY AND HOW IT EFFECTS THE LEGITIMACY OF YOUR COMMUNITY

Privacy has always been a concern among consumers. *Transparency* is a relatively new concern. It refers to the source of the information being clearly posted or shared. Concerns with transparency have been brought about by the rise of what many in the press today refer to social media.

The term *social media* was coined in 2004. Social media consists of the online tools and platforms that people use to create and share opinions, insights, experiences, and perspectives with each other. Social media is not limited to text; it can include images, audio, video, and a mix of all of those things. Today, the most popular social media are blogs, message boards, podcasts, and wikis. Social media have allowed consumers who generate the content to hide or minimize their relationship with the products they talk about in the content they post. That is the nature of transparency—whether the content creator is clear about his or her relationship with companies that they talk about.

Consumers who receive information from social media often assume that many of the messages they receive emanate from consumers who are unaffiliated with marketers. Let us say, for example, that you regularly read a blog (a Web log), sort of an online diary, from someone you do not know who is interested in something you are interested in, like fishing. Let's assume a friend of yours told you about the blog, or you discovered it one day when you were surfing the net for fun. One day you are reading the blog, and the blogger starts talking about a new line of fishing lures she has recently purchased and enjoyed. As a reader of the blog, do you think that the blogger found out about the lures by accident, random shopping, or surfing the net? Or do you think the blogger was paid by the manufacturer to write about the lure on her blog? Most of us would assume the former, but increasingly often, it is possible that it is actually the latter.

Think about it. If you trust someone, anyone, you will have a specific type of trust in the information that they provide. With our fishing lure example, you may be more likely to try out the new lure if you trust the source of the information, the fisher who writes the blog. How would you feel, then, if you found out that the only reason the fisher writes about the lures is that she was paid to do so? This is an example of a complete lack of transparency in a communication situation.

Social media channels rely on deeply trusted relationships among consumers. Therefore, you must exert special care and attention when using social media, including email, when communicating with your customers to prevent any possibility of confusion or deception. Consumers must get enough information to understand what they are seeing and where it came from. This may sound pretty basic, but you'd be surprised at how many marketers try to disguise their identity when using word of mouth.

Examples of Digressions in Transparency

Some examples of word-of-mouth practices that were lacking in transparency that you have might have heard about include programs from top marketers and entertainment companies.

- In 2003, Sony Ericsson hired sixty actors in ten cities to accost strangers and ask them, "Would you mind taking my picture?" Those who obliged were handed, of course, a Sony Ericsson camera phone to take the shot. After the strangers took the picture, the actor would remark on the benefits of the device.
- Vespa scooters hired models in Los Angeles to ride around to hip night spots on the scooters. Once at the night spots, the models flirted with patrons and provided them their phone numbers for future contact. As it turns out, the phone number connected the patrons with information about where to buy a Vespa scooter.
- A video posted on YouTube by someone named Lonely Girl generated huge amounts of views as most visitors thought the videos were an actual online diary of a free-spirited teenager from a conservative household. After several installments of her video diary were aired, it came to light that Lonely Girl was an actress and her video diary was filmed by aspiring filmmakers.

None of these interactions are technically deceptive, at least not deception as defined by the FTC, because there is no material harm in the interaction. That is, people were not spending money for a product based on false information. However, learning the truth disappointed many, who felt they were taken advantage of by situations they thought were real. This may have some repercussions for all marketers in the future. Consumers overall can become more wary about the messages they receive; trust in companies can be diminished, and sales can suffer.

THE WORD OF MOUTH MARKETING ASSOCIATION PRINCIPLES OF WOM MARKETING

To address this issue before it becomes out of hand, the Word of Mouth Marketing Association (WOMMA) is establishing principles for word-of-mouth marketing. WOMMA, recall, is the official trade association for the WOM marketing industry. The Association's mission is to promote and improve word-of-mouth marketing. It believes in protecting consumers and the industry with strong ethical guidelines, promoting word of mouth as an effective marketing tool, and setting standards to encourage its use. You can learn more about WOMMA at their Web site, www.womma.org.

WOMMA has created what it calls an honesty policy that has three major components. These are great guidelines for you to follow for any type of word-of-mouth communication you engage in.

- Honesty of Relationship: You say who you are speaking for.
- Honesty of Opinion: You say what you believe.
- Honesty of Identity: You never obscure your identity.[1]

In order to make sure that all of your efforts, either in word of mouth or for your community, are as transparent as possible, consider the following.

1. Make sure you disclose your relationship to the person receiving the message in every message. Do not assume that once they have signed up for your mailing list you can stop reminding them of your relationship. People today get so many emails and other messages that it cannot hurt and can only help to reinforce the relationship you have.

   Suggested language: "You are receiving this mail/email from *<store name>* because you indicated to us that you wish to receive it. If you no longer wish to receive it, please let us know by emailing *<email address>* or calling *<phone number>*."

   Place this message at the bottom of every email or paper mail you send out. For email, you can place it in your signature file so you do not have to remember to type it in every time you send something out.

2. Make sure the information you are sharing with your audiences is honest and authentic. Indicate your sources (i.e., from manufacturers or suppliers, or from the creator of the product) whenever possible.

   Suggested language: instead of saying, "Blonde hair is the 'in' color for the season," say "The creative artists at Matrix have told us that the newest trend in hair color is blonde, blonde, blonde."

3. Use your identity in every communication you send, and have everyone who communicates with your customers use their identity also.

   Suggested language: Start messages with "Good morning, this is *<your name>* from *<your store>* and today's message is about . . ." If others in your store send messages, be sure they indicate their relationship to the store also. "Hi, this is Francis from *<your store>*. You might see me working behind the cash register in the back of the store, or updating the stock in the housewares department. I want to tell you about . . ."

4. Do not use false or misleading subject headings in either your emails or your online posts. There's been a lot of talk about the value of mystery in some online communications. Some companies post fun videos about their products on YouTube without any type of corporate identification. One recent example was a video of an inventor who made a Mini Cooper automobile into a robot. The video looked like it was shot by an amateur videographer. Viewers of the video wondered who the inventor was and what exactly he did. It caused many people to debate the video online and to work to discover the actual source of the video. When people found out that the source was Mini Cooper's ad agency, Crispin Porter and Bogusky, reactions were mixed. Many viewers were happy they found the source of the video, but others were disappointed that what seemed to be an amateur video was actually a corporate commercial.

SUMMING UP

In this chapter, we have shown you

- Why you should have a privacy policy.
- How to craft a privacy policy.
- The importance of transparency in communications.
- How to make sure transparency is achieved.

Being an ethical communicator is simple: You should treat your customers and your staff in the ways that you yourself would like to be treated. If you feel that a message may be problematic, for whatever reason, think about why you have that feeling. Ask yourself if you are comfortable with friends and family seeing every message you send out. If you are not, why not? What can you change to make yourself feel comfortable? Is there anything in your message that you'd be embarrassed to discuss publicly? If a reporter called you up and asked you about your business practices, would you be proud to discuss them?

It is also important that you respect and honor the rules of media channels that you use. Some Internet providers will have specific terms of service that you should be aware of before you start to send out messages. For example, the terms of service may suggest that you cannot send spam or violate specific privacy rules.

In sum, it all goes back to one of the first things we talked about in this book: knowing your customers. If you have a clear understanding of who they are, what they are interested in, what they like and do not like, you should have an easy time communicating with them and becoming part of the social media that they use on a regular basis. When you put your customer at the center of everything you do, you will most likely end up doing the right thing. And when you do, you'll reap numerous benefits in many ways.

Chapter **11**

The Adventure Begins

Thank you for going on this journey with us! We hope we have provided you with tools, information, insights, action steps, and ideas to get started with word-of-mouth marketing and customer communities. We know there is a lot to consider, and we hope you are eager to get started on your journey. Your adventure is just beginning.

Where to begin? With an action idea, of course. As a final action idea, we offer these suggestions on getting started using some of the ideas in this book.

Customers

Take a moment to review your current practices in collecting customer information, and try one new way of learning about your customers. For example, try an online poll, a focus group, or a mail survey. Combine the information gleaned from this new technique with your existing knowledge, and review it all with a fresh eye, given what we have talked about in this book.

Conversations

Today, begin having informal conversations with your customers. Find out what they like, and what you might be able to improve in your store and in their shopping experience. Most important, encourage every customer to start the word-of-mouth process by asking them to tell their friends about the things they like about your store. Thank them in advance for becoming part of the conversation.

Community

Think about your current Internet presence and make plans to improve it. If you don't have an Internet presence, call up your cable company or a local Internet service provider to see about getting an online presence.

Commitment

Commit to repeating these steps every month or so, integrating other aspects that we have shown you throughout the book as you see fit.

Once again, we ask you to revisit your marketing grid. At this point:

- See how word of mouth fits in with your traditional advertising.
- Set goals in terms of your word-of-mouth activity for an upcoming period (three months, six months, or a year, it's up to you).
- Identify when you might be able to start your online community, and set a grand opening goal on your marketing grid.
- Identify how employees will help you with these efforts.

You have not heard the last from us! We want to hear about what you do—what works, what does not. It should not surprise you that we have set up a community where readers of this book can share their experiences and learn from others. We will also have a lot more information at the community site that we were not able to fit into the book. We will be there, too, to answer questions and help out in any way we can. Visit www.underdognetwork.com and look for the link for those who have read the book. We will ask you to register with some basic information and then you will be able to join in with the community. We look forward to seeing you there!

Appendix

Your Local Store Marketing Toolbox

This special section is designed to provide you with some basic, hands-on instruction to implement some of the suggestions we talk about in the book.

- Toolbox 1: Developing Your Marketing Grid
- Toolbox 2: Creating a Map to Discover Your Trading Area
- Toolbox 3: Using ZIP Code Tabulation to Think about Your Local Market Area
- Toolbox 4: A Primer on Demographics
- Toolbox 5: Data-Collection Techniques
- Toolbox 6: Talking to Customers: What to Ask
- Toolbox 7: Analyzing Data
- Toolbox 8: Collecting Data on Your Web Site

TOOLBOX 1: DEVELOPING YOUR MARKETING GRID

Purpose: The purpose of the marketing grid is to allow you to visualize your marketing plans for the upcoming year (or some other period) in order to determine optimal windows for word-of-mouth marketing activities.

Implementation: One basic way is to create a simple table or grid with three or four columns and about twenty rows. You will organize your advertising and marketing plans using the rows to indicate the months of the year, and the columns to track your sales plans and your traditional advertising efforts. So set up a table or grid and then:

1. Input your planned sales and promotions and the types of traditional advertising that you will use to support them.
2. Add a column that will give you space to plan how you will integrate word of mouth and customer community activities in this annual plan.
3. Use the grid as you move through the different chapters in this book to keep track of ideas as you develop them.

For example, your next three months of advertising might look something like this:

- January: End-of-year clearance ad running in the newspaper on January 1, Valentine's Day teaser ad on January 28.
- February: Radio promotion for Valentine's Day, February 1–14.
- March: Easter promotion (radio and newspaper), March 15–30.

Using this information, your grid might look, at this point, like Table A-1.

Then, as you add activities that you discover and create through your travels through this book, your grid might start to look like Table A-2.

Table A-1 Preliminary Promotional Grid

Month	Promo	Media	Word of Mouth: Target	Word of Mouth: Activity	Community: Target	Community: Activity
January						
Wk 1	End of year	N				
Wk 4	Valentines	N				
February						
Week 1–2	Valentines'	R				
March						
Week 3–4	Easter	R, N				

Table A-2 Promotional Grid

Month	Promo	Media	Word of Mouth: Target	Word of Mouth: Activity	Community: Target	Community: Activity
January						
Week 1	End of year	N	Family	Email about final clearance specials		
Week 3				Valentine's Day sneak peek		
Week 4	Valentine's	N			Message board	How do you celebrate Valentine's Day?
February						
Weeks 1–2	Valentine's	R	Friends and Flirts	Send Valentine's Day cards		
March						
Week 2			Store Champions	Referral event: spring trend fashion show	Message board	What's your must-have accessory for spring?
Weeks 3–4	Easter	R, N	Family	Poll: what summer items are you thinking about?		

TOOLBOX 2: CREATING A MAP TO DISCOVER YOUR TRADING AREA

Purpose: A Map will allow you to visually identify your own retail trading area.

Implementation

1. Find a local map. Identify the location of your store on the map.
2. Identify on the map the key shopping areas in your community. These key areas will include any local malls, the large grocery stores, popular strip malls, and other destination sites that generate a lot of traffic.
3. Look at how close these places are to each other, and estimate an area around each to estimate a trading area for each of those sites (see Figure A-1).
4. Pinpoint your store location on the map, and look at the general area that you fall in, and have an idea of your local trading area.

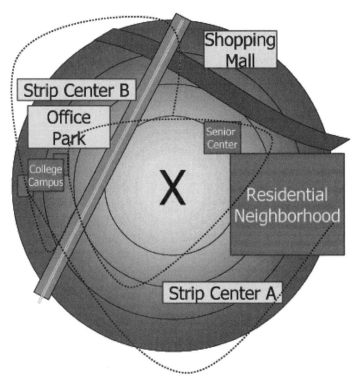

Figure A-1 Local Store Map

TOOLBOX 3: USING ZIP CODE TABULATION TO THINK ABOUT YOUR LOCAL MARKET AREA

Purpose: ZIP code tabulation allows you to use information that you have collected about your customers to fine-tune your local trading area information.

Implementation

1. Identify what customer ZIP code information you currently have on file. If you have your customers' names and addresses on file (if you own a video rental store, for example) you can simply calculate the frequency of visits by ZIP code. For other types of businesses, ZIP code tabulation can often be built into your point-of-sale machines and then downloaded into a spreadsheet for analysis. Alternatively, you can also have a clipboard at every register where your employees manually tally the visitors' ZIP codes and time of day that they visit.

2. The next step is to develop a spreadsheet that tallies the ZIP codes of your customers. Once ZIP code information is collected, it can be put in a spreadsheet or manually tallied to identify the numbers of customers coming from each ZIP code. Then, you can calculate the percentage of your total customers that come from each ZIP code. This is illustrated in Table A-3. Once you have your percentages, you want to identify the top 75 percent of your customers; this is your primary local trading area.

3. The final step is to use the data for making decisions. Once you have the ZIP codes, you can look at the relationships between the people living in the ZIP code and your business. You can also look at the proximity of your customers to your competitors. If we use the 75 percent rule, we would determine that for the example above our retail trading area consists of persons living in ZIP codes 97403 and 97405.

Table A-3 ZIP Code Tabulation Spreadsheet

ZIP Codes	Customer Count: Week of 11/1	Percentage of Total Customers
97401	45	9
97402	27	5
97403	220	47
97404	34	7
97405	153	31
94530	3	1
54672	1	<1

An alternative method: If the thought of tallying ZIP codes on a spreadsheet is daunting, you can use a local map and pushpins. Place pushpins at the approximate addresses of each of your customers. This gives you a visual sense of where they live, and you can even count the pushpins to create a table similar to the one above. This is especially useful for those areas with high population density in a single ZIP code.

TOOLBOX 4: A PRIMER ON DEMOGRAPHICS

Purpose: Demographics provide wonderful snapshots of your customers. However, many demographic reports use a lot of terminology and lingo. This toolbox is a primer on what different demographic terms mean and why it is important for you to know about these measurements. The best place to get demographic data is from the U.S. Census Bureau, online at www.census.gov.

Population and Households

What it is: The basic units of most census data are (1) the total population of people two to eighteen years old, (2) the total population of adults eighteen years old and above, and (3) the number of households. *Population* is defined as all persons living in a geographic area. Households consist of one or more persons who live together in the same housing unit, regardless of their relationship to each other.

How you use the data: Tracking changes in population over time can help you determine what types of general changes are happening in your market area. If it is growing—if, for example, the total population and/or the number of households have increased over five years—then your business should be growing as well. If population is declining, you may need to extend your local trade area in order to maintain your business.

Most households have a primary shopper responsible for most of the purchases made for the household. However, other members of the household can have input on the purchase.

Income

What it is: Household income is the total amount of money earned by everyone in the household and is a good indicator of spending power of residents.

How you use the data: In most cases, the more income a household has, the more it will spend. Thus, targeting these homes may be beneficial to your business. Keep in mind, though, that income is not always the best predictor of what people will buy and how often they will buy those things. For example, travel agencies have found that there are three types of travelers: completely price-sensitive (who are always looking for deals), value-conscious (who like a deal but will also pay for certain amenities), and non–price-sensitive customers. Household income is not a good predictor of who will fall into which group, so do not rely on household income alone for your decisions.

Education

What it is: Education describes the level of formal education that individuals achieve. Demographic data segment people into groups based on whether they have a high school education or not, as well as the level of post–high school education that they have achieved.

How you use the data: Education is often tied to income because in many cases, individuals with higher levels of education often have higher incomes than those with less education. Because they are so closely tied, many retailers ignore educational level when making decisions for their store. Exceptions include bookstore, computer, and software stores. If your store includes these types of products, consider education in your plans.

Age

What it is: Age demographics examine differences in groups who are younger and older.

How you use the data: Age is an important factor to consider because personal expenditures change as an individual ages. For example, drug stores flourish in areas with a large senior population. Toy stores, day care centers, and stores with baby-care items are successful in areas with many children and infants. Clothing stores and fast food establishments thrive in retail areas that contain a large concentration of teenagers, college students, and other young adults. Understanding the age of your population can help you fine-tune your product or service mix.

Occupation

What it is: Demographics differentiate between persons with white-collar occupations and blue-collar occupations.

How you use the data: Many retailers use the concentration of white- or blue-collar workers to chose appropriate products and services for their store. Specialty apparel stores thrive in middle to upper-income areas and above-average white-collar employment, while do it yourself–type stores may be more successful in blue-collar areas.

Ethnicity

What it is: Segmenting customers based on their race.

How you use the data: Retailers that use segmentation based on race and ethnic groups must make sure their efforts are authentic as well as accurate. Correct assortments, fashion orientation, advertising media, and product selection are all influenced by ethnicity. We discussed this much more in Chapter 6.

Housing

What it is: Assessing whether people in the trading area own or rent their homes and whether they live in single-family or multi-unit homes.

How you use the data: The number of homeowners and the rate of housing turnover is an important factor for numerous retailers. People who own their own homes will spend more on home furnishings and other items for their homes.

TOOLBOX 5: DATA-COLLECTION TECHNIQUES

Purpose: There are many ways to collect information about your customers. Some you may have tried, some may be new to you. This toolbox gives you an overview of all the different data-collection techniques and discusses which loyalty segment (the Family, the Flirts, or the Phantoms) may be most likely to respond to the technique. Consider these techniques and decide which may be right for you.

Phone Surveys

- Basic tactic: Collect data by phone
- Best for: Family and Flirts

With a phone survey, customer information is collected via telephone by calling customers the week after they visit your store. During this phone call, you can see what they particularly liked about their visit, what they did not like, and what they would like to see added. This technique requires that you get their phone number while they visit your store. Some customers are reluctant to provide this information as they are worried they will be called unnecessarily or the information will be misused. You can overcome this by telling them that you will be calling occasionally to see how you can better serve them. You can also offer a gift or a coupon to the customers that offer to be called for the survey.

The benefits to the phone survey are that the personal touch of the phone call gives your customers the feeling that you care about their business. These types of surveys are relatively inexpensive, especially if you have employees who can make some of these calls as part of their jobs. They can be straightforward to analyze. The biggest drawback is that it takes a lot of time to conduct the surveys, and you may wish to hire professionals who can conduct them consistently so the same questions are being asked of all participants. You also cannot ask in-depth questions with a phone survey, as people are not likely to want to spend a lot of time on the phone with you.

Card Surveys

- Basic tactic: Customers fill out preprinted cards containing your questions
- Best for: Family and Flirts

Using a single card (the size of a postcard) that contains five or six questions is an excellent option for conducting research. In addition to the questions, the card should allow sufficient space for customers to write in their responses. This card can be filled out either while they are in your store, or after they have left. In the latter case, the card should have prepaid postage so customers can mail the card back to you.

The benefits to card surveys are that you can collect information from many of your customers and collect this information very quickly. Card surveys do not require many staff members to implement, and they are fairly easy to analyze. The biggest drawback is the limited number of questions that you can ask, but this can be overcome with the creating of a few key questions that give you the information you need. Additionally, the cost of card surveys is a bit more than the cost of phone surveys, as you need to pay for printing and return mailing of the cards.

Online Surveys

- Basic tactic: Customers answer survey questions online
- Best for: Family and Flirts

Online surveys allow customers to visit the survey and answer the questions at their leisure. There are numerous free survey programs that are available online (visit www.underdognetwork.com). Once you have set up your survey, all you need to do is promote it to your customers. You can have your point-of-sale system include a message on the bottom of receipts, or you can hand customers a card with the Web address and ask them to take the survey. Again, you might consider offering some type of incentive to people once they complete the survey. Most survey programs allow you to send out an email to respondents, which they can then print out and bring to the store on their next visit.

The benefit is that you can collect data very quickly and inexpensively. The programs are very easy to set up, and all you will need is a bit of time and money to promote the survey. You will also collect email addresses of your customers, which you can use to start a word-of-mouth program (we talked about that in Chapter 4). The drawbacks are that you will eliminate any responses from people without an Internet connection, and you will miss that personal touch from a phone survey.

Mall Intercepts/Personal Surveys

- Basic tactic: Pass out your survey at places where large numbers of customers gather: malls, movie theaters—any place other than your store!
- Best for: Friends and Phantoms

The mall intercept consists of collecting data via a paper survey that you pass out randomly to customers at a public location, such as a mall or a movie theater. It is one of the only ways to potentially reach the Phantoms. What you will do is get permission from the mall to pass out the surveys, and then randomly select people to answer the written questions for you. You will need many copies of the surveys as well as a supply of paper and pencils for your respondents.

Alternatively, you can hire surveyors to ask the questions to the individuals and record their responses.

The benefits to this type of survey are of course that you reach many more people than your regular shoppers. You reach them immediately and fairly inexpensively. You can dedicate a day or two to collecting data. However, this will take a bit more time than the other types of surveys.

Focus Groups/Group Discussions

- Basic tactic: Invite a small number of shoppers to a discussion about your store and your competitor's store
- Best for: Family, Friends, and Phantoms

Focus groups are a totally different animal than the other types of surveys that we have outlined. They are not really surveys at all. Instead, a focus group is an extended conversation with a small group of people (say, eight to ten). You will want them to talk about their experiences and impressions of your store and of your competitor's store. You can invite customers from your store and ask them to bring along a friend (maybe someone who does not shop at your store). Again, some type of incentive is important for focus groups, since it is likely that the participants will commit about an hour or an hour and a half of their time to the process.

This may seem simpler than other methods, but in reality focus groups are a bit more complex from a logistical standpoint and from an analytical standpoint. You will need a space to hold the focus group, like a conference room or a private room at a restaurant. You will need an experienced facilitator to lead the discussion and to analyze the results. You will need tape recording equipment to record the proceedings.

The information you will get through this technique will be much richer than other techniques, but it will be more expensive and take a bit more time to collect.

Regardless of the method you select, you should conduct customer research at least twice a year, more frequently if you are experiencing flattening sales or even a decline in sales. Your customers can provide insights about your operation that your sales numbers cannot show you.

TOOLBOX 6: TALKING TO CUSTOMERS: WHAT TO ASK

Purpose: Once you have determined the best way to collect data about your customers, you need to formulate some specific questions that you ask all of the participants in your data-collection process. This toolbox will help you in that regard.

What to Ask: Short Surveys

If you can only ask five or six questions (i.e., a phone survey or a card survey), consider asking some of these questions in an open-ended format (i.e., provide a blank space where customers can write down their responses). These questions can also be used as some of the initial questions for a focus group discussion.

- Where do you shop for *<items offered by your store>*? For services: Please name the different *<restaurants, hair salons, etc.>* that you have visited in the past three months.
- Approximately what percent of your *<category>* budget do you spend at *<your store>*?
- What do you like about *<your store>*?
- What do you like about the other stores you shop/restaurants you visit?
- What could we improve at our store?
- Do you tell others about the store? Why or why not?

Here is an example for a women's shoe store called Shoe City. Your questions would look like this.

- Where do you shop regularly for shoes?
- Approximately what percentage of your shoe budget do you spend at Shoe City?
- What do you like the most about Shoe City?
- What do you like about the other shoe stores where you shop?
- What would you like to see us change or improve at Shoe City?
- Do you tell others about Shoe City? Why or why not?

Figure A-2 shows a longer survey, which was designed to be used to talk to visitors at a store but can also be used as a mall intercept survey or, with some modifications, as an online survey. Consider integrating some of these questions into your data-collection practices at your store.

Figure A-2 Telephone Customer Survey

This survey assumes you have collected the name and phone number of customers through some means at your store, and that you are contacting them via phone for a follow-up visit. You could easily adapt this survey for an online survey or even a mall intercept in person survey.

Begin survey by saying: *Hello/Good morning or Good afternoon. May I please speak to [name of guest]? My name is _____ ; I am owner of [your store] that you visited recently. We are currently conducting a survey with all of our current and new guests. Would you have a moment to talk about your last visit to [your store]? I won't take more than ten minutes of your time.*

If the customer says yes, thank them and continue. If they say no, ask if there is another time that might be more convenient, or thank them and say goodbye.

As you ask these questions, do not hesitate to probe for reasons why the customer feels the way he or she does. Use phrases like "Can you tell me more about that?" or "what happened?" to learn more information about their visit.

(1) What did you purchase during your last visit?
   _____

(2) How did you feel about your purchase when you left the store? And later when you were back at home?
   _____

(3) Do you feel that the money that you spent equals to the value of service or product that you purchased?
   Yes.
   No. Explain _____

(4) During your visit, did the staff seem knowledgeable?
   Yes.
   No. Explain _____

(5) Can you remember the name of the member of our staff who worked with you ?
   _____

(6) How was the visit to the store in terms of your time?
   Did you feel hurried or rushed?
   No
   Yes (Explain) _____
   Did you feel it took too long to complete your business?
   No
   Yes (Explain) _____
   Was it just about right?
   Yes
   No (Explain) _____
   _____

(7) What do you like best about coming to [your store]? _____

_____

_____

(8) How could we serve you better? [If the customer does not know, probe as to whether the store could be cleaner, friendlier, have a greater variety of products]

_____

(9) Would you recommend [your store] to a friend or family member? Why or why not _____

(10) Do you have any other comments or suggestions that can help our store serve you better? _____

End the survey by saying : *"Thank you so much for your time."*

TOOLBOX 7: ANALYZING DATA

Purpose: Analyzing the responses is a somewhat detailed process that involves tabulation of responses. If you have used multiple choice questions, you should tally the number of responses to each answer choice in order to see what the most popular answers to each question were. However, many of the questions we suggested that you ask in Toolbox 6 are considered open-ended questions where the people answering the surveys are free to write as much or as little as they wish. This toolbox shows you how to analyze those responses.

Implementation

1. One way to start is to set up a system where you have a separate piece of paper for each question. As you read through the open-ended questions, write down quick notes on what people are saying, and then add some type of notation to indicate the frequency of the response. For example, the first time you read that a customer likes the friendly and helpful employees, write down "friendly helpful service" on the first sheet ("what do people like about us?"). Then, when you read this on additional surveys, put a star or a slash mark next to the phrase to keep track of the number of customers that believe that also.

2. Keep an open mind in grouping the data, and try to be as broad as possible so you will not end up with too many categories that make analysis difficult. For example, if one person wrote down that they like your friendly helpful service and another wrote down that she likes your fast service, you might want to tally both of these under a broad service category, and just keep notes on how different customers define service. Creating too many categories will slow you down and will make it hard for you to make decisions based on the research.

3. At the end of your research, you will have a list of things about your store that people like and dislike. You will also have numerous suggestions on changes you can make. With your star or slash mark system, you will also know how strong those feelings are.

TOOLBOX 8: COLLECTING DATA ON YOUR WEB SITE

Purpose: It is extremely important to gain a clear view of what your visitors do on your site. You will want to examine how many visitors are coming to your site, what pages they are visiting, which of your articles people are reading, and what tools they're using most. You will want to understand which page visitors are exiting from your site, so you can better refine your content and keep them engaged.

To gauge the effectiveness of your marketing, you want to know where they are coming from to get to your site: from a search engine result, from a link referred by a friend, or by typing in your URL directly, because your Web site is now "top of mind."

This kind of information is available by viewing your Web statistics or activity reports, and this toolbox is designed to help you identify how to get that information. You will leverage this information to make better decisions and refine your site content.

Implementation: Depending on your Web hosting service, you are probably paying for these reports as part of your hosting package. Check with your hosting service and see if you are getting the reports, and request them if you are not already getting them. You should familiarize yourself with the level of tracking currently offered by your Web host at no additional fee. Ask the representative at the hosting company to walk you through a report or two to make sure you understand the data that they provide.

1. Examine your visitor reports to see how often people are visiting. Look at changes on a monthly basis to see if the things you add to your site are attracting new and/or more frequent visits.
2. Track the specific pages that people are visiting and include some of your key word-of-mouth stimuli (such as email alert signups or "send this page to a friend" links) on those pages.

In addition to the information available from your hosting service, you can gain access to more insights by purchasing or subscribing to a third party service offering in-depth reports. These subscription services vary in monthly cost, from free to under $30. They are a valuable bargain to give you detailed traffic reports that really put you in the driver's seat in understanding visitor habits. These third-party solutions do all the heavy work for you—you need only paste some code on your pages and later log in to view reports that you can sift and filter to meet your needs.

Here are some links to subscription stat packages that you can use for free or for a nominal monthly fee:

- www.w3counter.com
- www.sitestats.com/home/home.php

- www.clicktracks.com
- www.opentracker.net/index.jsp
- statcounter.com

There are also more sophisticated Web reporting tools and software you can purchase when your site is heavily visited or if you are conducting e-commerce and want to analyze in-depth shopping behavior. This will require a larger up-front investment.

When you are interested in these more robust reporting tools, just do a search for "Web traffic analysis." If you would like to learn more about the intricacies of Web statistics and analytics, visit www.underdognetwork.com.

Notes

Chapter 1

1. McPherson, Miller; Smith-Lovin, Lynn; and Brashears, Matthew E. "Social Isolation in America: Changes in Core Discussion Networks over Two Decades." *American Sociological Review* 71 (2006): 353–375.

2. Keller Fay. "Keller Fay's Talktrack Reveals Consumer Word of Mouth Features 56 Brand Mentions per Week," 2006. Available online at www.kellerfay.com/news/Talkrack5-15-06.pdf.

3. The Verde Group. "Tall Tales about Problems When Shopping Turn-off Friends and Colleagues," 2006. Available online at www.verdegroup.ca/default.asp?action=article &ID=37.

4. Terdiman, Daniel. "Buzz Marketing Firm Rakes in $13.8 Million," 2006. Available online at news.com.com/Buzz-marketing+firm+rakes+in+13.8+million/2100-1024_3-6027175.html?tag=nefd.top.

Chapter 2

1. Center for Community Economic Development. "Downtown and Business District Market Analysis," 2006. Available online at www.uwex.edu/CES/cced/dma.

2. Reichheld, Frederick, and Teal, Thomas. *The Loyalty Effect*. Cambridge, Massachusetts: Harvard Business School Press, 2001.

3. Ibid.

4. Ibid.

Chapter 3

1. GfKNOP. "Word of Mouth Ain't Just Blogging," 2005. Available online at www.gkfnop.com.

2. Rosen, Emmanuel. *The Anatomy of Buzz*. New York: Doubleday, 2000.

3. WOMMA Research and Metrix Council. "WOMMA Terminology Framework." In *Measuring Word of Mouth*, edited by Andy Sernovitz. Chicago: Word of Mouth Marketing Association, 2005.

4. Ibid.

5. Carl, Walter. "Mapping The Conversational Geography of Word of Mouth Marketing." In *Measuring Word of Mouth*, edited by Andy Sernovitz. Chicago: Word of Mouth Marketing Association, 2005.

6. Marin, Rick, and Boven, Sarah Van. "The Buzz Machine." *Newsweek* (July 27 1998): 22–26.

7. Lazarsfeld, Paul; Berelson, B.; and Gaudet, H. *The People's Choice*. New York: Columbia University Press, 1944.

8. Keller Fay. "Keller Fay's Talktrack Reveals Consumer Word of Mouth Features 56 Brand Mentions Per Week," 2006. Available online at www.kellerfay.com/news/Talkrack5-15-06.pdf.

9. WOMMA Research and Metrix Council. "WOMMA Terminology Framework."

10. GfKNOP. "Word of Mouth Ain't Just Blogging."

Chapter 4

1. FrequentFlyer.com. "History of Frequent Flyer Program," 2006. Available online at www.frequentflier.com/ffp-005.htm.

2. Maritz Loyalty Programs. "Customer Loyalty Clarified." Marketing Poll, 2004. St. Louis. Available online at www.maritzloyalty.com/loyalty-mlmpoll.asp.

3. Aaronson, Jack. "Reward Programs: Common Strategies," 2005. Available online at www.clickz.com/showPage.html?page=3509491.

4. Ibid.

5. Aaronson, Jack. "Rewards Program: Interval Schedules," 2005. Available online at www.clickz.com/showPage.html?page=3519926.

6. IPC. "Customer Retention: Keeping Your Best Customers for the Long Term," 2005. Available online at www.incentivecentral.org/Customer_Retention__Keeping_Your_Best_Customers_for_t.568.0.html.

7. Jantsch, John. "Referral Marketing: The Most Powerful Form of Advertising," 2006. Available online at www.ducttapemarketing.com/referral_marketing.htm.

8. Plesh, Doug. "Referral Marking-Having Others Work for You," 1997. Available online at www.asha.org/about/publications/leader-online/archives/2003/q2/030429e.htm.

9. Jantsch. "Referral Marketing: The Most Powerful Form of Advertising."

10. Maritz Loyalty Programs. "Customer Loyalty Clarified."

Chapter 5

1. McPherson, Miller; Smith-Lovin, Lynn; and Brashears, Matthew E. "Social Isolation in America: Changes in Core Discussion Networks over Two Decades." *American Sociological Review* 71 (2006): 353–375.

2. Mayer, R. C.; Davis, J. H.; and Schoorman, F. D. "An Integrative Model of Organizational Trust." *Academy of Management Review* 20 (1995): 709–734.

3. Ganesan, S. "Determinants of Long-Term Orientation in Buyer-Seller Relationships." *Journal of Marketing* 58 (1994): 1–19.

4. Bedbury, Scott. *A New Brand World*. New York: Penguin Books, 2002.

5. Markman, Jon D. "Starbucks' Genius Blends Community, Caffeine," 2005. Available online at moneycentral.msn.com/content/P107679.asp.

6. Bedbury. *A New Brand World*.

7. Anonymous. "Coffee House? Bank? It's Getting Harder to Tell them Apart." *Bank Marketing* 38 (September 2006): 3.

8. Brady, Diane, and McConnon, Aili. "Booking a Room in Cyberspace." *Business Week* 4000 (2006).

9. Wolf, Alan. "The Focus Is on Females at Best Buy's Studio D." *Consumer Electronics* 20 (2005): 22.

10. Duque, Federico. "Innovation and Development: The Customer Is Always Right." *KM Review* 8 (2005): 4-4.

11. McConnell, Ben, and Huba, Jackie. "Creating Customer Communities: A Surgical Approach," 2003. Marketing Profs.com.

12. PR Newswire. "Making Social Networking Work for Marketing," 2006.

13. Umstead, R. Thomas. "Seeking User-Generated Romance." *Multichannel News* (2006): 17.

14. LeFever, Lee. "Customer Communities: Negative Feedback Can Be Your Friend." *Common Craft* (2005).

15. Algesheimer, Rene, and Dholakia, Paul. "Do Customer Communities Pay Off?" *Harvard Business Review* 84 (2006).

Chapter 6

1. Smith, Donnavieve; Menon, Satya; and Sivakumar, K. "Online Peer and Editorial Recommendations, Trust and Choice in Virtual Markets." *Journal of Interactive Marketing* 19 (2005): 15–37.

2. Hampton, K. "Living the Wired Life in the Wired Suburb: Netville, Glocalization and Civic Society." University of Toronto, 2001.

3. Wellman, B.; Haase, A. Q.; Witte, J.; and Hampton, K. "Does the Internet Increase, Decrease, or Supplement Social Capital?" *American Behavioral Scientist* 45 (2001): 436–455.

4. Calabres, A., and Borchert, M. "Prospects for Electronic Democracy in the United States: Rethinking Communication and Social Policy." *Media, Culture and Society* 18 (1996): 249–268.

5. McConnell, Ben, and Huba, Jackie. "Creating Customer Communities: A Surgical Approach," 2003, MarketingProfs.com.

6. Coleman, J. "Social Capital in the Creation of Human Capital." *American Journal of Sociology* 94 (1988): S95–S120.

7. Williams, Ruth, and Cothrel, Joseph. "Four Smart Ways to Run Online Communities." *MIT Sloan Management Review* 41 (2000): 81–91.

8. Cothrel, Joe, and Williams, Ruth. "Understanding Online Communities." *Strategic Communcations Management* (February/March 1999): 16–21.

9. Preece, Jenny. *Online Communities: Designing Usability, Supporting Sociability*. New York: Wiley and Sons, 2000.

10. Hessan, Diane, and Schlack, Julie Wittes. "Online Communities: Public V. Private." *Brandweek* (May 15, 2006).

11. Figallo, Cliff. *Hosting Web Communities*. New York: John Wiley, 1998.

12. Dutta-Bergman, Mohan J. "The Antecedents of Community-Oriented Internet Use: Community Participation and Community Satisfaction." *Journal of Computer-Mediated Communication* 11 (2005): article 5.

13. Kim, Amy Jo. *Community Building on the Web*. Berkeley: Peach Pit Press, 2000.

14. Smith, Satya, and Sivakumar. "Online Peer and Editorial Recommendations."

15. Miezkowski, Katharine. "Are You on Craig's List." *Fast Company* (2000): 26–30.

16. Cothrel, and Williams. "Understanding Online Communities."

17. Williams, and Cothrel. "Four Smart Ways to Run Online Communities."

18. Preece. *Online Communities*.

19. Donalth, Judith. "Identity and Deception in the Virtual Community." In *Communities in Cyberspace*, edited by P. Kollock and M. Smith. London: Routledge, 1999.

20. Ibid.

Chapter 9

1. Sennet, James. "Clusters, Co-Location and External Sources of Knowledge: The Case of Small Instrumentation and Control Firms in the London Region." *Journal of Planning Practice and Research* 16 (1) (2001), 21–37.

2. Boyd, Danah. "Friends, Friendsters and MySpace Top 8: Writing Community into Being on Social Network Sites." *First Monday* 11 (December 2006). Available online at www.firstmonday.org/issues/issue11_12/boyd/index.html.

3. Lenhart, Amanda, and Madden, Mary. "Social Networking Websites and Teens: An Overview." Pew Internet and American Life Project, 2007.

4. Boyd, Danah. "Identity Production in a Networked Culture: Why Youth Heart MySpace." St. Louis, MO, 2006.

Chapter 10

1. Word of Mouth Marketing Association. "WOMMA Ethics Code," 2006. Available online at www.womma.org/ethics/code.

Index

Page numbers followed by "t" indicate material in a table.

About the Authors

STEVE O'LEARY is CEO of O'Leary and Partners, an advertising agency in Orange County, California. In his thirty-five-year advertising career, he has worked on over twenty retail brands that range from single-store operations to large chains, from dry cleaners to fast-food restaurants. His clients have included Coca-Cola, Miller Brewing, Century 21 Real Estate, and Taco Bell. He has been a speaker at various industry events and client conventions and workshops and a guest lecturer at numerous universities.

KIM SHEEHAN is associate professor at the University of Oregon, where she teaches classes in communications and advertising. She spent twelve years in the advertising industry, working with fast-food clients such as Wendy's and McDonald's, and with retail store clients like Kinney Shoe and Laura Ashley. She is the author of *Controversies in Contemporary Advertising* and a coauthor of *Using Qualitative Research Methods in Advertising*.